Dedication

This book is lovingly dedicated:

> To my nieces,
> Jennifer, Katherine and Laurel Williams
> and to others of their generation –
>
> > I hope that by better understanding death,
> > you may more fully live;
>
> To Esther and Jerry Hicks, and Abraham,
> for daring to venture into the leading edge,
> and inspiring me to the next level;
>
> To Hermaden,
> For your wisdom, love and patience,
> And our evolving journey.

ISBN: 978-0-9854284-5-7

ISBN-10: 0985428457

Library of Congress Control Number: 2014953640

Hermaden Press
Lafayette, Indiana

First print edition, Oct. 2014
First e-book edition, Jan. 2013

I can see you.
I can hear you.
I can see your light.

From my mother,
a few days after her re-emergence

Contents

Author's Note

I realize that people have many names for what they consider The Divine. In this book, I refer to the force of divine intelligence and unconditional love as God. It is a name with which I am comfortable. Yet it is not a term with which everyone is comfortable, or which fits everyone's spiritual or religious beliefs. In the same way, I use "Heaven" as the name of the non-physical place where we reside before we are born and to which we return when we die. When I refer to God or Heaven in this book, please substitute whatever names or words you prefer. As Shakespeare wrote, "A rose by any other name would smell as sweet."

Section I: A Re-introduction to Death

Chapter 1
Understanding Death

I invite you to consider a new perspective on death. Or perhaps it will not be new to you: perhaps it will resonate with you deeply. But intentionally deciding to spend time contemplating death, at least long enough to read a book on the subject, means that you are seeking a better understanding. That usually happens when death has made an entry into one's life...often, an unwelcome entry. Most people don't pick a book on death to read simply because they are curious. Or bored.

We all have people in our circle of family and friends who have special expertise. These are our "go to" people. If I have a question about my car, I go to Joe. I have other friends with expertise like computers, music and baking. In my circle of friends, I am the "go to" person on death.

Like many people in their fifties, I have dealt with a lot of death in my life. My parents, my husband, my grandparents: all have died. Aunts and uncles, dear friends and beloved companion animals have all departed their earthly lives. I have seen many changes in the course of their living and dying, including much illness and dementia.

I have also seen strong faith and spiritual belief: people who believed they and their loved ones were going to a better place when they died; people who believed in the soul and in a powerful God; people who loved and believed in the power of love.

I have been interested in death most of my life. I wanted to know all I could about death. I studied different religious traditions and spiritual philosophies. I listened to many personal stories about death, dying, and near-death experiences. I talked to people who communicated with the dead. And I had many first-hand experiences with people who were preparing to die.

3

Death is a part of everyone's life. It has been a big part of mine. I set out to study it the way most people seek to earn a college degree. I wanted a diploma in death. I wanted to understand it as fully as I could without actually dying yet.

As I learned more, I discovered that most people had questions about death, too. I could get many pieces of this jigsaw puzzle of "understanding death" to fit together. This puzzle is fun for me. Some people search for the great mysteries of life. To me, one of the biggest mysteries of life is death – something we each will experience, something that touches every one of us if we live on this planet.

This journey of discovery has led me to some very unexpected results. I found first that I had to suspend what I thought I knew about death – what I learned in my religious upbringing, which was Christian. I also had to suspend some of the traditional views the church taught about God. Yes, God is a huge part of death, but not in the way I had been taught as a child. I had to get rid of preconceptions and open myself to new approaches.

In school, we are often taught to find a hypothesis and then look for information to support it. But what if you open yourself to the answers, first? Ask the question and *allow* the answer. It seems simple enough. But one must allow all possibilities. If you really want answers, you can't look just for the answers you want. You can't look only for the answers that fit neatly. Allow the answers, and then see how they fit together. Do they fit together? Ask and allow. Ask and allow.

I will be the first to say that I don't have all the pieces yet. I think some of the pieces may be impossible to see, or understand, when we are looking at death from an earthly perspective. But what I have found is that I have enough pieces of the jigsaw puzzle that my picture of death – the picture that has gradually been coming together for many years – has been of value to the people I know. And that is why I am writing this book. Maybe others will find it of value. Maybe my nieces will. Maybe there are people who can look at the pieces I have put together and continue the puzzle after I am through working with it.

I have been struck by how often the fear of death, and a misunderstanding of death, can impede one's life. The lack of knowledge can bring devastating pain. Death is something we all deal with. Doesn't it make sense we would try to understand it – *really* understand it?

I hope this book helps on your journey of understanding.

I also want to be clear: I am sharing what I have come to believe about death. I am not asking you to believe it. It is up to you to choose what you believe. This book shares my choices, my understanding.

What My Parents Taught Me

My parents used to explain that the spirit is like a hand. The body is like a glove. When we are born, the spirit goes into the body like a hand into a glove. When we die, the hand leaves the glove; the spirit leaves the body. The hand still exists.

When we bury or cremate someone, we are only disposing of the glove. We are not disposing of the real person: the spirit. The real spirit of a person is what we come to know and love.

We may also love the body of someone, for it is the exterior cover of how we picture and conceive of that person. It is often the body that we touch or hold. But that image of someone, that person's body, is the glove and not the hand. It is the body our loved one lived in, but it is not the person that we loved. It is a representation of our loved one, but it is not the actual being. Each person's glove is unique when living on earth, because each person's spirit is unique.

5

When we die, it is like the hand goes out of the glove – the body – and reunites with the larger body of that person in the non-physical realm, in Heaven. When someone is alive, we see and interact with the hand of that person in the glove. But the wholeness of that person is much larger. The hand is an extension of that person's consciousness, but it is not that whole, entire person.

God

Imagine the sun. Most of us are taught in elementary school that the sun is a powerful body of energy that gives off light that shines on the earth and other planets in our solar system. The sun is not a closed, contained body. It emits energy. It emits the light that we see every day. Even though we are far away from the sun physically, it still shines, lighting and warming our world.

When we see the sun in the sky, that is what we think about: what we see in the sky. We do not often consider how powerful the light is that radiates from the sun. It is this energy that lets us have our days. It is when our portion of the earth is turned away from the sun that we have our nights. The sun still shines at night – our portion of the earth is just turned away from it. The sun is always brilliantly shining, always emitting energy and light.

Yesterday was a cloudy, rainy, cold day: one of those early autumn days when you want to drink something warm and stay cozy inside. Today when I woke up, the sky was blue and the sun shone brightly. The sun is shining, I thought happily. It felt like all was right with the world, and it would be a sunny day in every respect.

Except the sun was shining yesterday, too. The sun shines the same on a cloudy day as it does on a sunny day. From the sun's perspective, every day is a sunny day because the sun shines brightly every day.

What was different yesterday were the weather patterns on the part of planet Earth where I live. There were weather patterns yesterday that involved clouds and rain. So I did not see the day as sunny because I could not see the sun. But the sun was shining just as brightly yesterday as it does today. It was actually the light from the sun that let me see the gray clouds yesterday. What I prefer is seeing the sun in a way that feels more direct to me.

Now, God is like the sun. The sun shines all the time. God shines love all the time. But sometimes I can see it and sometimes I can't. When I don't see the sun shining on a rainy day, it is not because the sun has stopped shining. It is just that I don't see it. I don't focus on it. From my earthly perspective, I think a cloudy day is not a sunny day. And it is true: they are different kinds of days in the way that I experience them. Except the sun is shining brightly on both kinds of days. I just am not giving my attention to the sun. Yesterday, I was giving my attention to the clouds and rain and cold. The sun was still shining brightly behind those clouds, but I was focusing on what I perceived as the dreariness of the weather, not on the fact that the sun was still shining.

If my part of the planet had been experiencing a drought for a long time, I might have thought the rain was wonderful and welcome. I might have thought that a rainy day was absolutely the best kind of day to have. Now, my part of the Earth is not experiencing a drought. It is becoming winter here. And while there are many things about winter that I appreciate, there are also many things about the contrast of winter I do not appreciate. So I not only saw yesterday as a dreary day, but as an indicator of more dreary days to come.

Yesterday the sun was shining as brightly as today. God was shining love brightly yesterday and today. The difference for me was where I was directing my focus. I gave my attention yesterday to the clouds and the cold: not to the sun, not to the fact that the sun always shines. This morning, it was easier for me to recognize the sun was shining because the day was bright and beautiful by my standards. But God loves just the same today as yesterday. The sun did not shine less brightly or brilliantly yesterday. I just decided that it was not a beautiful day.

God loves all the time. That is who God is. Because I am not focused on the brilliance of that love does not mean God is loving less. God can not, does not, love less from one moment to the next. God's love is constantly expanding and growing. God's love grows brighter, more brilliant and beautiful, with each moment that passes.

Choices

I get to choose where I direct my attention and my focus. I can focus on the clouds or on the fact that the sun is still shining. I can focus on the fact that someone I love is no longer in his or her body, or on the fact that my loved one's spirit has reunited with the larger body of who he or she is and is still very much alive. I am the only one who can control my thoughts: what I choose to think, and where I choose not to give my attention. These are my choices.

I make these choices constantly. But I may not always recognize that I make these choices constantly.

When we are children, we are often taught by the grownups around us to focus where they direct their attention. Adults work hard to make the subjects of their attention become the subjects of our attention. Have you ever seen a young child playing in a place where all the grownups were worried or sad? It might be a funeral home, a hospital, a courtroom, a country where people are at war. The grownups are feeling strong negative emotion. The child wants to play. And the grownups are hushing the child, telling the child to stop playing, stop having fun. The grownups think that the child doesn't understand the seriousness of what is going on. But maybe it is the child in these situations who could be teaching us. Life goes on. We can direct our attention to things that feel good in any situation.

We see the same thing with animals that live with us. The human feels sad. The dog brings a ball to the person, wanting the human to throw the ball and become playful. The dog is inviting the person to have a different thought, a better thought. But the human will often scold the dog and tell the dog to "leave me alone" with those negative thoughts. The dog is saying, "You don't have to be sad. Come play with me." And the human is insisting on feeling miserable and rebukes the dog. This is one of those cases where we have to remember that old saying: dog is simply g-o-d spelled backwards. The dog is playing the role of God in this situation, lovingly inviting the human to a place that feels better. That is also what the child is doing. Both are indicating to the humans around them that they do not need to feel bad. There are choices about where we direct our attention. And we make those choices all the time.

Dealing with death in a way other than our society has taught requires that we choose to think differently about it. We need to be open to pondering it. We need to ask questions and allow answers. We don't need to be afraid. To the sentiment that death and taxes are inevitable in life, I would say: only death is, ultimately, inevitable for all of us. And that is not a bad thing.

Would a loving God really create something bad for all of us to endure? Or is it that we do not understand death the way God created it to be? Do we understand God the way God really is? Has society shaped our view of death to fit its model of appropriateness and profit? Making people afraid of death has had profound benefits for some in our society – and many negative consequences for others. Fear is a substantial motivator. But love: *love inspires*. God gave us "death" to allow us to continue to grow and change and have wonderful experiences. God gave us death out of love: not wrath, revenge, or judgment. Death is a way we can continue to expand. Death is a way we are guaranteed periodically to reunite with our higher selves, to assume a new perspective, to allow ourselves to embrace the fullness of God's love even if we have cut ourselves off from it for decades.

Death is the gift of a loving God

Chapter 2
Understanding Energy

You might ask me, "Why do you have a chapter on energy? I want to learn about death, dementia and the soul." If you don't understand a little about energy, the rest won't make sense to you. So I am just covering the basics here: essential, general concepts.

I

Everything is energy. We are energy. The cells of our bodies are energy. What we call "the soul" is energy. Everything and everyone we see around us is, at its essence, energy. We are taught this in school in our science classes. But we somehow fail to translate this understanding to our more practical, everyday lives.

We also emit energy. And we receive energy. We all read energy to varying degrees, even if we don't call it that. We know that hearing is receiving waves of sound and interpreting it. Seeing is receiving waves of light and color that our brains interpret. All of our senses are reading and interpreting energy. From my front porch, I can hear the movement and sounds of vehicles that are blocks away, even if I don't see them. I know what those sounds are. If I hear a sound I am not familiar with, I perk up and wonder what the sound is.

Have you ever encountered someone who looked fine but seemed upset to you? The person may have smiled and told you everything was fine. But you were reading the energy. You knew that person was not okay, even if the person looked all right and said so. You could feel something was off.

II

Energy has a range of frequencies. We learn this from listening to radio stations. Each station has its own frequency. You adjust the dial on your radio according to the music you like, to find the station you want to hear. If all radio stations broadcast on the same frequency, the sound would be muddled and unpleasant. We couldn't differentiate one station from another. Different stations operate on different frequencies.

Energy is the same way. The energy you emit has a frequency. You will tune into other aspects of life that are occurring in similar frequencies. Music stations on the radio are grouped by frequency. Classical music stations are close in range, as are religious stations. Country music is in another range; rock and pop are in other ranges. We know this. We know the placement of their frequencies is not random.

If I am traveling and I want to find a classical station, I can tune to the frequency of my home classical station. There may not be a station at this exact frequency that I can receive, but there will be other classical stations nearby on similar frequencies.

Different emotions have different frequencies. Different thoughts have different frequencies. Different activities have different frequencies.

III

Energies attract other energies that are on the same frequency. Likewise, you are more comfortable with other people that are on frequencies similar to yours.

Have you ever gone to a party or social event and noticed how people group together? People are most comfortable with other people who are like them, who share a common frequency. You may find yourself drawn to someone, then find out you have something in common. Maybe you are going through a similar life event: having experienced a recent death, or preparing for a wedding, or having children with something alike. The people with whom you resonate the most will usually have – not just an interest in common, but an energetic frequency in common with you.

People who "rub you the wrong way" are usually operating on a very different frequency than you are. If you value honesty, you will not feel comfortable with someone who lies – even if you don't know for a fact the person is lying. If you are sad, a happy person may seem annoying or, at the least, insensitive. If you are a playful and energetic person, a deeply depressed person may seem to be in a different universe. In essence, you are in different energetic universes. You may have trouble relating, or may feel like this person is drawing you "down." You are living on different frequencies.

You may have heard of a principle called the "law of attraction." This is a universal law that *like energies attract.* If I am focused on grief, then I will likely tune into other sad things. I will find sad news on television. I will find grieving people when I am out socially. I will be drawn to books on grief. If I am living a joyful life, then I will miss the television news, or tune in to the one happy story they are covering that day. I will find myself drawn to other happy people. I will engage in activities that are fun.

IV

The Universe brings us more of what we give our attention to. This is a responsive, interactive universe. When we think about something, we are emitting energy on that frequency. When we watch television, we are emitting energy on the frequency of the program we are watching. When we talk with someone, the subjects we choose to discuss will activate those frequencies. Have you ever noticed that after you thought about someone you hadn't seen for a while, you hear from the person, seemingly out of the blue? Or perhaps you find the person's phone number when you thought you had lost it.

You talk to a friend about a special subject of interest or curiosity. Within a day or two, one or both of you have come across more information on that topic. You think, "What a coincidence!"

When we swim in water, we know we are "in" something. We can feel the water responding to our movements. If I push upward quickly, I create a splash. If I try to kick fast, I can feel the water moving out of the way of my legs. I know that the water is responding to me. I know my action will create a reaction with the water.

Our universe is the same way. When we think, we create. When we give our attention to something, we are offering a frequency to which the universe will respond. When we take action, we create a reaction on that same frequency. Everything is connected by energy. Swimming in the water, we can see and feel the water. But the energy of our world is just as alive, real and responsive.

V

When you have a fluid like water flowing in a stream, if something interferes with that flow, the water has encountered resistance. Resistance is something that interferes, that resists, flow. Boulders in a stream can cause resistance. Water naturally tends to find the path of least resistance, and will simply flow around the boulder. But humans will often look at the boulder and have negative emotion. We can become so focused on the boulder that we crash into it instead of simply going around it.

If I want something, but instead I focus on not having it, I am offering resistance to receiving it. If I want to feel good, for instance, but spend most of my time researching illnesses and wondering if I have them, then I am not focused on enjoying my physical well-being. I am spending most of my time on *not* enjoying well-being.

If I want to be happy but I spend most of my time watching television news stories about international tragedies, the abundant information about unhappiness can interfere with my ability to be happy.

If I want more money in my life, but I spend most of my time worrying about bills, then I am offering resistant energy to a greater flow of money.

Resistant thoughts interfere with the creation of what we want. We stare at the boulder in our path, instead of working with the flow of water, of energy, to take us around the boulder. We focus on the problem rather than the solution.

Thoughts that don't feel good are not aligned with the loving way that God sees the world or our situation. God is always looking from a broader, more expansive perspective. God sees the solutions and wants us to go there. God calls us toward those solutions, like a bird who is sitting in a tree, calling its babies to leave the nest and experience flight: over here, come here.

We all have resistant thoughts. We all offer thoughts sometimes that interfere with us tuning to the frequency we want. If you notice yourself doing this, just stop. Redirect your thinking. Don't be hard on yourself; be kind. Just redirect. Mentally, hit the "pause" button to your current pattern of thought. No catastrophe has happened. Just shift your thinking, intentionally, to a thought in alignment with what you want, that feels better. Thoughts that are resistant to what we want don't feel good. Find a thought that feels better.

The more we are aligned with God, with Source, the more allowing we become of what we want. The more allowing we become, the greater our flow and our ability to simply take the path of least resistance to what we want. We will be inspired to move toward what we want, toward what we are asking for.

Summary

➢ Everything is energy. We are energy. We also receive, emit and interpret energy.
➢ Different energies have different frequencies.
➢ Like energies attract.
➢ When we think, we create.
➢ What we give our attention to, we get more of.
➢ This is a responsive universe. Everything is interconnected.
➢ The fewer resistant thoughts I have and the more I am in alignment with God, the faster I can live a happier life.

Chapter 3
Building Blocks

Here are some of my beliefs, the foundational beliefs on which this book is based. I am sharing them here so we can build the experience of reading this book together.

Building Block One:
God is.

This book will not much make sense to you if you do not believe there is a God or a force in this universe equivalent to what I call God. What you call the Being that I refer to in this book as God may be something different and that is fine. Just substitute the word or name you prefer when you read "God."

The God I know is not the God some religions teach. The God I know is all-loving and loves everyone and all beings all the time. The love that is God is so powerful that it would have to be diluted many times in order for us to experience it fully.

Most religions underestimate God. This has always seemed ironic to me. Some religions teach a narrowly-defined, man-at-his-worst kind of God. The God I am writing about in this book is Love. God always loves. God always loves you. God loves you unconditionally. God never judges. God always sees the best in you.

God is much more immense than we can imagine from our human perspective. Because of that, we often try to make God more like us. But God is much greater, much more expansive than we can wrap our human perspective around. God is not just the most powerful loving force in the Universe. God is the life force. God is the life energy, the love energy, which flows through all of us, all the time.

God is always calling us, coaching us individually to be the best we can be. But God loves all the time, no matter how much we might be – or not be – in alignment with that vision. God is love in its purest, highest, most powerful form.

Building Block Two:
Each one of us has a unique perspective.

Each one of us has lived a different set of experiences that has shaped our perspective of the world. Each of our perspectives is unique. There are no two beings with the same perspective. No two people have lived exactly the same life. Each one of us is unique. Each one of us is special.

We may want different things in our lives and take different paths to get where we want to be. But the feelings we reach for are ultimately the same. We have that in common. We may want different things, but the *feelings* we seek are something we share.

We want to be happy. We want to be fulfilled. We want to feel free. We want joy. We want to love. We want to be loved. We want to feel good. Our journeys to reach these feelings may be different. But our goals of how we want to feel are similar.

Because each of us has a unique perspective and unique desires, God couldn't give us just one path to follow. There are many paths. We each have our own. Part of the fun of the journey is creating our own path.

Building Block Three:
God gave us internal guidance systems.

To help us achieve what we want and what God wants for us, God gave each of us a built-in guidance system. This system is comprised of our emotions and intuitive feelings. Our emotions help to guide us on the path to what we want. So does our intuition. Does something feel good to you? It is on your path. Does something not feel good to you? Then you don't see that experience as being on your path. The things that feel the worst to us in life are things that feel like they are departures from our paths, things that we perceive as dislodging us from making progress on our journey to what we desire. Positive emotions are indications that we feel we are moving toward what we want.

Negative emotions are indicators that we do not see something as helping us move toward what we want. Now, there are two parts to this. Negative emotions are indicators that we perceive something is not moving us toward what we want. But it can also indicate that we are not seeing a situation the way God sees it.

Negative emotions can indicate to us something we do not want to do or continue doing. But negative experiences can also clarify for us what we do want.

Death is a situation that brings most of us negative emotions. And most of these emotions mean that we are not seeing death as God sees it. Death is not a big deal to God, because God knows that we are eternal beings. We don't need to grieve over the loss of our loved ones because our relationships are eternal: we will be with our loved ones again. So when we feel negative emotion about death, it is because we are not seeing death the way God knows it to be. If we can see death the way God sees it, we will feel very differently about it.

Building Block Four:
We are powerful creators.

Every single one of us is creative. We create our own lives. We create our earthly experience.

I am always amused when someone – especially an older someone – tells me they are not creative. Often, this person has had a career and a family. There was a place they lived and decorated. They chose clothes to wear every day.

They may have picked out a type and color of vehicle many times. They chose topics to talk about with people. They celebrated holidays. They chose activities and hobbies. How could anyone not describe him or her self as creative? We make choices all the time, every day. We create our own lives. Even someone who lives in one room for many years makes hundreds, even thousands, of choices every day.

We are all creators. We choose our thoughts. We choose what we like and what we don't. We choose what we want to give our attention to and what we don't. We are active creators every moment of our conscious lives.

Building Block Five:
Earth is a playground.

I have heard many people talk about physical life on Earth as a school. We come here to learn, they say. We come here to have lessons.

No. Earth is a playground. It is a place we come to play. It is a place we come to co-create with others through a physical experience.

Now, does that mean we don't learn?

Of course not. Learning is inevitable. Growth and expansion are inevitable. But we came here because of the fun we knew we could have on this playground.

I know many adults who would tell you some of their most painful childhood memories came from playground experiences. Others would tell you their best childhood memories came from playground experiences. Some would even say the best and worst of their childhood happened on playgrounds.

Playgrounds are places to play. Earth is a place to play. But while we do a lot of playing, playgrounds are also places where we co-create the experience of play with others. And those interactions are very mixed, and often very meaningful.

20

We may play by ourselves sometimes. We may play with others sometimes. We will no doubt have a diversity of experiences on this playground, as we intended. We will no doubt learn a lot through that variety of experiences. But the intent is to play; our intent in coming here is to have a good time. We want to co-create a playful, joyful experience.

Building Block Six:
God loves us and wants us to be happy.

God loves us. YES! God loves *you*. YES! God wants us to be happy in our experience here on earth. YES! That is why God has sent so many spiritual teachers forward, to remind us of why we are here and how we can reclaim happiness.

Our existence here on earth contributes to the expansion of the Universe. As we experience contrast and determine preferences – find things we like and things we don't, things we want less of and things we want more of – we are creating new thoughts, new energies. The expansion of NEW is necessary for the health of the Universe. What is brilliant is that expansion is also inevitable. Growth is a by-product of the way God created the Universe. The Universe – and *we* within this Universe – will always continue to expand because that is the way God created it. Genius!

Building Block Seven:
What we call "death" is a natural part of this expansion.

"Death" is a part of the inevitable process of growing and recycling.

There is no end to us. There is no "death" in the sense that death is an ending.

Death is simply a part of our continued expansion. The state we call "death" simply provides us with a new window, a new vantage point, a new perspective from which we can continue to experience life.

The concept of "endedness" is foreign to the flow of energy that God generates in the Universe. There can be no endedness, no state of being ended. God is about flow. The flow of energy is constantly expanding. Death is a part of this expanding flow of experiences God gives us.

Think about the flow of water in a river. The water doesn't just "end." It doesn't stop being because it reaches the geographical end of the river. Something happens to it. Maybe it spills into a larger body of water. Maybe water is siphoned off to irrigate farmlands or create reservoirs. Some may be diverted to smaller streams and creeks along the way. Some is evaporated by the sun and returns to our cycle of weather. There is no endedness to water. It changes. It undergoes a metamorphosis if it does not remain river water. But it always becomes something else, something more. It does not end.

We, like that water, do not end. Death is our metamorphosis. It marks a change for us, not an ending.

Building Block Eight:
We are expressions of consciousness that have taken the perspective of a physical body for this earthly experience.

The simpler way most people would say this: we are souls in physical bodies on earth.

That is not exactly right, but it is close.

Consider that the soul is a body of energy, and an extension of a larger body of energy. The physical body we come into is formed partially through the genes of our biological parents, but the energy of our soul influences it. And we are taking the channel, or perspective, of a physical body on planet Earth.

We are "born" into a physical body, but the soul is already in existence before our physical birth. We come in as physical babies, but our souls have already experienced many different perspectives and are very wise already. We live many lives here on earth. This current experience is just one.

These "expressions of consciousness" do not begin and end with the experience of one physical body. They – we – are timeless.

Another word for "soul" is "spirit." We are spirit: spiritual beings. And we are having a physical experience through the gift of our bodies here on earth.

As with the example of a hand extending into a glove, there is a larger body to which we are attached. I refer to this body as our God-self. A part of me is here, on earth. But the bigger part of me is in the non-physical world. That bigger, fuller version of me is my God-self. The biggest part of the God-self is always non-physical. The hand of the body may extend into earth, but the biggest part of that soul body always remains in heaven.

Building Block Nine:
There is no "death."
The spirit/soul is eternal.

What we call "death" is simply the soul changing perspectives. The soul changes perspective from a physical body having an earthly experience. The soul does not end. The soul simply changes perspective.

Heaven is our home. Heaven is the non-physical dimension where we spend most of our time. It is where we reside before we come into this physical dimension. It is where we go when we leave this physical perspective. Home is the place we always go back to.

Heaven is where we are closer to God – not because we can't be closer to God on earth, but because we usually develop many false beliefs on earth that keep us from being closer.

Heaven is where our God-self resides. Everyone has a God-self. The God-self is what some people call our higher self, our ideal self, our guardian angel, our inner being, our higher power, our authentic self. There are many different terms for it. It is the part of us that resides in heaven and maintains the perspective of God about us. Our God-self keeps its non-physical perspective even while we are here on earth. It is a part of us that always keeps a loving perspective. It is always calling us to stay connected with God and with the way God sees things. Our God-self always loves us. It calls us to be happy and fulfilled.

Building Block Ten:
Looking from a Broader Perspective

It is important to look at our lives – and deaths – from a more expansive viewpoint, the way that God does. One human life on earth, placed within the context of eternity, does not seem very long. That life may seem long to us here, while we are living it. But imagine it instead within eternity.

Imagine looking through a camera lens. I can zoom the lens in to make an object far away seem very big and very close. Or I can zoom it out and see that object as part of a much larger scene.

Just as we can change our perspective, so God can, metaphorically, zoom in and out. God can see the sparrow's nest in one tree, or God can see the whole forest. But God always knows that, even while looking at that one tree, the tree is a part of the forest. The forest is part of a larger eco-system that expands to include our whole planet. Everything is connected, and inter-connected.

We forget that. God doesn't. It is important, when we are looking at death, to look from a broader, more expansive and comprehensive view. One perspective changes to another. The larger perspective enhances the closer view we experience.

If I am saying a temporary good-bye to a loved one who is dying, I need to remember: this is a short-term departure. The physical separation is short-term. Indeed, I need to remember that my loved one's soul is not dying and will still be very much alive after his or her "death." We will be together again. In fact, we can still enjoy each other's company after he or she has left the perspective of the physical body.

We need to see the big picture. Grief comes from a close-up view. God knows there is no separation and no death, so sees no reason to grieve.

Chapter 4
The Nature of the Soul

Death is a withdrawing of consciousness from the physical body; it is a change in focus. We move our viewpoint, our perspective, from the physical body back to a fully non-physical perspective.

A stream of consciousness – of creative life force – flows from our God-self to the physical body. This stream of consciousness is what we call the soul. The soul is not a physical mass. It is a stream of energy. I have talked with people who envision the soul like an invisible football of magical energy that comes into the body when we are born and sticks around while we are alive. "Death" is supposedly, in this viewpoint, what occurs when the soul leaves. But this is not accurate. The soul is a stream of energy. It flows to us continuously while we are in our physical bodies. The depth of the stream – the amount of energy flowing – varies during our lives. When we are born, we are not calling a strong stream of energy forward yet. What is coming into and through this new body is adapting to the body's physical nature, and the physical nature of this new experience. It is adapting to the energy of earth and the environment into which we are born.

When we are thriving at life – when we are happy and eager and passionate – we call more energy forward. When we are not, we are not calling forth as much. You know what it feels like when you feel "fully" alive – when it feels like you are highly energized and every cell in your body feels present and happy. You also probably know what it feels like when you feel less well, less happy, and you feel like your energy has diminished.

As people grow older and approach death, often the energy in this stream diminishes. There is still a stream flowing, but it is not a bountiful stream like a person may have experienced earlier in life. As people are in states where their bodies are older and their physical conditions have declined, often their streams are calling forth less energy. *Growing older does not need to be this way, but for many, it is.*

When a person dies, there is no longer a stream coming forth. The stream does not flow into the body anymore. The stream of consciousness is still alive. The person is still alive. The stream is simply not flowing to the body anymore. There is not energy coming forth from the non-physical realm into the perspective of the body.

The stream still exists. The source of the stream still exists. But the stream no longer flows into the body for a person to have the experience and perspective of a physical body here on earth.

The soul is this stream of energy and consciousness. This stream is coming from the non-physical level into the physical body. When someone dies, the stream still is. It just "is" on the non-physical level. It doesn't flow into the body, but it still flows. When people are in heaven, they are still these streams of energy and consciousness. The amount they call forward still varies somewhat, but not as much as when we are here on earth.

In heaven, we don't experience the "negative" aspects of earthly life. We are never as unhappy in heaven as we are here on earth. When we are in heaven, we don't experience the resistance to that flowing stream to the extent we can here. For many people, the best days lived on earth are closer to what is "everyday" in heaven.

When people die and lose the aspect of themselves that has been resisting the flow of energy here on earth, they experience a rush of energy and well-being. Think about a river that has been blocked by a dam. The dam may let a certain amount of energy through. But it doesn't let anywhere near the amount of water through that wants to flow. The dam holds water back. That's what a dam does. So, when we die, if we have been blocking energy from flowing vigorously to us, then it is like the dam bursts. There is no longer a dam diminishing the flow. We are fully ourselves – the water that is our stream flows vigorously to us. It is part of the "rush" many people experience when they die. They stop thoughts that are resistant and block the stream. The dam their thoughts has created breaks free and they are experiencing fully the flow of who they really are. How wonderful that feels!

What most people call the soul is the part projected here, into our physical perspective. But this is only part of the much larger stream of consciousness that is who we really are, in our fullness.

A greater understanding of the soul will unfold in the course of this book, as you come to understand the depth and power of who you really are.

Chapter 5
Putting the Pieces Together

Death

Death is a return to our home. Our home is the non-physical realm many of us know by the name of "heaven." It is a place of love, acceptance, and joy. It is not a "reward" for years of suffering on earth. No one earns the "right" to go to heaven. It is ours before we come to earth and ours when we leave earth. We all go there.

We do not, however, just go as we are on earth. On our journey there, we leave behind all the patterns of thought and action that keep us from fully embracing joy and love on earth. Those actions and thoughts are not part of our essence. We have picked them up during our time on earth, and we leave them behind when we die. There are no murderers or "sinners" in heaven. Those aspects of someone do not belong in heaven, and they stay behind, here on earth. The best aspects of who we are: that is what we take with us to heaven. Everyone has "best parts," best aspects. Even if they have been separated from us for a long time, they still exist. We rejoin them at death. We remember them. We allow them. Heaven calls forth the best in us. And we all have "best" in us. Every single one of us.

People who have had near-death experiences can tell you they feel a lightness when they leave their bodies. They feel like they are shedding all worry and anxiety. They are emerging into a place of total unconditional love and acceptance. They experience a powerful love and sense of well-being that surpasses anything they have known on earth. Many don't want to come back. It is a strong, idyllic feeling. Knowing the way it really is, however, can also be a tremendous buoy once you are back. You know there is nothing to fear. No matter what happens on earth, in the end it all works out great. Wow.

Dementia

Dementia is a bridge between physical life on earth and re-emergence into the non-physical realm (the transition into heaven at death). When we are on earth, many of us develop patterns of thought that separate us from our true selves. We forget we are spiritual beings having the experience of a physical body and life on earth. We forget that we come from a place of total love and acceptance, and we return to it when we die. We forget that there is nothing to worry about. We forget that we are worthy, just as we are. We forget that God is a loving God who lovingly welcomes us with open arms, unconditionally and non-judgmentally, back into our "home" when we leave our bodies. We forget that we don't need to be afraid of dying: that it is a joyful transition. "Death" and re-emerging to the non-physical realm are blissful experiences of returning to a state of unconditional love where we leave all negative emotion and thought behind.

Dementia exists because we forget who we really are. Dementia exists because we fear. Dementia exists because we misunderstand death and God. Dementia exists because we worry we have to control everything, and we try so hard to control.

Dementia allows a gradual release of worry, fear, and control. Dementia is an easing of the thoughts that have confined us mentally.

Forgetting is a way of releasing. It is a way of returning to a place of allowing greater well-being. It allows us to allow a more peaceful death. It allows us to focus on the present moment, instead of the past or the future.

The Soul

The larger part of us is in heaven, and a part of us extends from heaven into a physical body on earth. But a part of us is always in heaven and never comes to earth. That is what people call by names like the higher self, the God-self or higher power.

Think about holding a flashlight that is turned on. The flashlight is being held by the larger, non-physical part of you in heaven. It shines the flashlight into a physical body here on earth. When you die, you are simply returning to that non-physical part of you. You change perspective from an earthly physical body to your non-earthly non-physical body. You return to the part of you that was holding the flashlight.

This analogy is not perfect. But you need to consider that you are Light, and the source of your light remains in heaven while you are on earth. When you die, you simply return to the source of your light.

Summary

Death is when we return fully home. It can be a reminder of the joy we have when we are united with God. It urges us to stay aligned with the love of God. It reassures us that if we wander from that alignment, we have a return to it guaranteed.

Death is meant to be a comfort to us – not a threat, punishment or source of grief. It is bliss. It is euphoria. It is a return to a love greater than most of us have known on earth. It is unity with God, and a return to that unity.

Our internal compass, undisturbed, will always point to God and to the unconditional love of God. Our thoughts and our attention to unpleasant things moves the needle from its true North, its true alignment. Leave the compass alone – don't disturb it – and it will naturally point us back to God.

It will always return us there, every moment of every day, if we do not provide interference.

Once you fully appreciate that you come from joy and you return to joy, it is difficult to become distressed about this earthly journey in-between.

Section II: Questions

Chapter 6
Questions Answered

This section contains questions that have been asked about death, and answers I believe to be accurate. Even if you don't agree with all of them, I hope they will propel your own thinking and understanding forward.

«« Q »»
What Happens When I Die?

Before I answer this question, I will ask you to try an experiment with me that will better prepare you for an answer. (You can't do this exercise if you are driving right now. If you are listening to this as an audio book and driving, please skip this question and return later.)

This exercise works best in a room with multiple places to sit. They don't have to be chairs: they could be places on a floor, a desk, or they might include several different chairs. You just need a variety of places where you can sit.

➤ Look around the room you are in and find several different vantage points. There may be places that are higher and lower, closer and farther: just places that will allow you different perspectives.

➤ Find an object you can view from all of those vantage points. You don't have to be able to see the object easily from all of those perspectives; you just need to be able to see the object. You might pick a piece of art on the wall, for example, or a photo on a desk. If you are outdoors, you can easily do this – just find a physical object to look at that you will be able to see from multiple perspectives: a tree, a sign, a patch of grass or cement, flowers, etc.

➤ Now move to the first vantage point and look at your object. Spend a couple of minutes noticing different details about it. Pay close attention.

➤ Move to your next seat, your next vantage point. Again, spend several minutes studying the object you have chosen. Notice anything that seems different about it from this vantage point and your first perspective.

➤ Move to your next perspective and do the same thing. Again, notice what is similar and what is different from your changing vantage points.

Now, think about the various ways your common object appeared from each unique vantage point. Perhaps the lighting changed depending on where you were seated. Perhaps different colors or aspects stood out. Maybe the object seemed smaller or larger to you depending on how close you were to it, or whether you were seated high or low. With each new perspective, the object probably seemed to change, even subtlety.

Now I will move more directly to the question at the head of this chapter. The traditional way of thinking about life and death is to think that we are a spirit. When we die, our spirit leaves our body and goes to the non-physical world, to what many people call heaven.

In reality, what happens is that our perspective changes: our vantage point moves. We did have the vantage point of a physical body living an earthly experience. At death, our vantage point changes: it returns to the non-physical world that we came from.

That means you can still see the same things you see now, the same people you see now. You will just be seeing them from a different perspective.

Instead of seeing the world from a physical, body-centered, earthly perspective, you will adopt a new, non-physical perspective. You are still you, but your vantage point shifts.

Think about this for a moment before you continue reading. It is really important that you understand this distinction before moving on.

You are still you. But when you die, your vantage point, your perspective, shifts. That is, simply and concisely, what death is. It is a change in perspective.

Expansive

When you die and assume a non-physical perspective, you are also opening yourself up to a much more expansive

39

experience and expansive world than you see now. You are not limited to the earthly perspective you are used to. There is much, much more to see and do. So while you can still see what is going on among your loved ones on earth, there is also a much more expansive experience to have. Your focus is not limited to earth, not limited at all. You are an expanded being when you die and assume a non-physical perspective.

When you die, you continue to be all that you are now, and more. So you continue to grow and expand when you die. In fact, if you have been experiencing any kind of limitation on earth, that limitation will immediately leave when you die and re-emerge into the non-physical plane. If you have a physical limitation, it will disappear. If you have a mental or psychological challenge, it will disappear, too. You will be completely whole. Any limitations will be gone. Think about that for a moment before continuing. Ponder what it would mean to you to be fully whole, without any of the limitations you have come to accept in this earthly realm. All of your earthly "baggage" is gone.

The moment you die, you feel freer, lighter.

All of your negative emotions leave you. You have nothing to be anxious or worried or sad about. People who are experiencing a lot of negative emotion on earth may feel a great sense of exhilaration. People who are already happy may feel happier. The extent to which you feel emotionally lifted will vary according to how you are feeling on earth when you "die." You will move to a place where you feel great joy. How much of a change that is for people varies on how they are feeling when they die. Some people feel a dramatic lifting emotionally: moving into a state of bliss from one of despair, for example. Other people, already happy, will not feel as dramatic a lift, but will still move into ecstasy.

"Peace" has different meanings for different people. Some people might describe the feeling of "being dead" as peaceful, but it is more joyful than a feeling of contentedness. Many people aspire to find peace in their earthly lives. But what you experience when you die is much happier than peace.

What you will also feel strongly is love: a powerful, all-encompassing feeling of love and appreciation. You will feel loved, and you will feel loving. You will be one with love.

You will have unlimited knowledge available to you. You can ask any question and get an answer. If you want to know something, just ask. You have access to divine intelligence.

You will still be you. But qualities of limitation will leave you. You will be happy. Anger will dissipate. Jealousy will dissolve. Negative emotions as we experience them here on earth will all be gone. You will look at the people you knew here on earth through eyes of unconditional love. Your stronger connection to your God-self, and your lack of resistant thoughts, will call the best of you forward and allow it to blossom. In death, we bloom.

««« Q »»»
How does it feel to die?

Death is sublime. You rise from your body and begin to ascend to heaven. You feel like you are answering a call, but you are answering willingly. You feel the presence and company of loved, loving beings.

There is an immediate lightness of being. All your worries, all your negative thoughts and emotions are gone. You feel free, whole, loved. The lightness of mind and emotion are exhilarating, energizing, rejuvenating. You feel yourself moving toward the most marvelous place that exists. You are happy, merging with pure joy and love.

You do not lose your individual perspective. You experience everything fully with your senses. Your physical body is where you left it, but you interpret everything just as if you still had functioning senses. You can communicate with other non-physical beings through thought, and they can communicate with you. You are returning home to a splendid place, an amazing state of being. There is an energetic heaviness you are leaving behind here on earth.

You feel the company of celestial beings that we on earth might interpret as angels, the name we have on earth for beings who bridge heaven with earth. They accompany us on this return trip home.

You feel such ecstasy, such bliss. The lightness is incredible. We often don't realize how much our thoughts on earth weigh us down. At the moment we die, we can feel the lift, the lightness. It is freeing.

You feel yourself becoming the fullness of who you really are: at one with your loving, wise nature.

You also find yourself thinking: *This is amazing, this is incredible. I can't believe I was worried. Everything on earth that seemed so troublesome now seems resolved and irrelevant. We were making such a big thing out of life on earth, and out of death, and this is wonderful. This may be the best part of earthly life, riding this current home.*

You feel embraced in a feeling of total love and acceptance, bliss beyond measure and words. You are pure joy, pure love.

Where do we go when we die?

The place we go when we die is what most people in our culture would call "heaven." Another word for "heaven" is "home." Actually, the dimension of life we are experiencing on earth right now is not our home; it only feels like that to most people. The place we spend the most time, eternally, is the dimension most people think of as heaven. Heaven is the place we go when we die. It is also the place we reside before we are born.

Heaven is not like earth: it is not a *physical* dimension in the way we think earth is. Still, it appears that way to us when we are there. We are still interpreting with what seem like earthly senses.

When we go to heaven, we leave our physical bodies here on earth. We appear in heaven as energy. If you look in the sky at night at a star and squint your eyes, you see a body of light. That is the easiest way to describe how we appear: a body of light, of energy. When we are in the non-physical dimension of heaven, we find it easier to interpret energy. Many of us don't use those abilities here on earth much – or we don't think we do. But our spirit, our soul, appears in heaven as a body of energy – not a physical body. From a heavenly perspective, this body of light is quite physical.

Yes, your friends and family will be able to recognize you – and you will be able to recognize them. But you will be recognizing their energy, not their physical body.

As you leave your physical body and re-emerge into heaven, you leave behind your physical body. You also leave behind all of the worries and anxieties associated with your physical life on earth. Earthly matters that might have meant a great deal to you, like paying your bills or caring for physical possessions, don't concern you anymore. Any negative emotions that you have been experiencing leave you. You will immediately feel a lightness of being.

You will emerge into positive emotions – and only positive emotions. People who are in great distress on earth immediately find a powerful sense of exhilaration and joy. People who are already joyful on earth will find a more expansive joy.

When you re-emerge into heaven, you are coming home. You aren't lost; you don't need an "orientation" session. You are coming back to a place you know very well. You may have forgotten about this place during your life on earth, but it is immediately familiar to you as you re-emerge.

Perhaps in this life on earth you lived in a home for a long time, or had a home that was meaningful to you, like your parents' or grandparents' home. If you left it and went back many years later, you still remembered basics: you knew the layout, you knew the "feel" of the property. That's how it is when you re-emerge into your heavenly home. You know you are home again. You feel you are home again.

There is no one to cast judgment on you about whether or not you get in. There is no punishment awaiting anyone. You are coming into a place where you are closer to God's love – where you are not resisting it the way most of us do here on earth.

You feel loved and accepted.

You know you belong.

You feel free.

You are free.

Heaven is heavenly. Heaven is home.

When you are in heaven, you feel expansive. You *are* expansive. You don't feel limited in the ways many people do here on earth.

You also have a broader perspective. That means you will be looking at people and situations more from a macro, as opposed to a micro, perspective. Things that don't make sense to you now will make perfect sense to you. You will see things more with the broad vision that God has. You will have an eternal perspective, as opposed to one that is more limited, situated within a smaller stance of time and space.

Any negative opinions you have of people will be gone, because you will be seeing them more as God does. You will see them within a larger perspective and have greater understanding of the things they did and the reasons they did them. Petty things that were very meaningful to you on earth will fall away; you won't care about them anymore.

There are no bills to pay in heaven. You don't have to worry about the cost of fuel, or keeping a job. Everything you want and need is there and readily accessible to you.

There is so much to do there, and you have as much time as you want to do these things. In heaven, there is a sense of timelessness. It is not a space-time reality like earth. You can travel to all the earthly places you want to see. You can check in on planet earth with the people you love and care about. And remember that there are many people already in heaven who are looking forward to your arrival, who will be glad to see you.

You can come back to earth when you want to. You can remain in heaven and just "visit" earth or you can choose to be reborn and come back in a physical body. The earthly dimension is still available to you when you are in heaven. Being reborn in a physical body on earth is something that you get to choose. We have all been here many times before because we wanted to be.

You create your life in heaven like you do on earth: through thought, through focus, through choices. But it is a more conscious, more aware choosing than most of us practice in this life on earth. Our choices are coming from our own broader perspective.

We also have a greater sense of interconnection in heaven: with each other, with all of life. There is no sense of separation or isolation.

Perhaps the greatest joy in heaven is our stronger connection with God and with our God-self.

«« Q »»
What is the relationship of the spirit to the body?

When considering the relationship of the spirit to the body, it is worth considering the hermit crab. The hermit crab does not birth its own shell in a traditional sense. Rather, other sea creatures have shells which they discard. The hermit crab finds one that is suitable and attaches itself to that. As the hermit crab grows, it discards the one it has been using and finds a newer, larger one that is more suitable for its expanded being.

The birth parents, that contribute the essentials needed for the creation of a physical body, create the physical shell. The spirit finds one that is suitable and desirable, and lives in it as long as the body serves the purpose. When it no longer serves the highest desires of a person, the spirit leaves that body.

Now, there is more going on here in the selection of birth parents than this analogy allows. But what is important to understand is that the body is like a shell. The hermit crab goes from shell to shell to shell, as it expands and has larger needs. So humans – and all living creatures – live in a body as it serves them, and discard the body when it no longer suits their purposes.

We do not confuse the essence of the hermit crab with the shell it uses for a while. Likewise, we need not confuse the spirit of a person with its shell, with its physical body.

We go from body to body, from lifetime to lifetime. We keep living. We survive. We thrive. Like the hermit crab, we are talking about the changing of a shell. Not death. Not a state of nothingness. There is no endedness to life.

The physical bodies left are regenerated by the earth into what is of value to those who continue to live here.

All spiritual bodies are eternal, evolving, ever growing and expanding. There is no endedness.

«« Q »»
Why are there so many different ways that people die?

When people are ready, for whatever reason, to make their transition from their physical body back to the non-physical perspective, the path by which they "die" is usually the path of least resistance. That means the path they take to "exit" the connection with their body will be one that is easily available to them. Sometimes, the path may seem logical; sometimes it may not.

The easiest way to think of the concept of "least resistance" is to think of water. When a stream of water flows, it chooses the path that is easiest. The stream finds a way to flow where it encounters the least resistance. When it finds resistance, or obstacles, in its path, it may go over or around them. It will choose lower ground over higher ground. The stream does not stop flowing because there is an obstacle in its path; it flows around, or through, the obstacle.

The stream of life does not stop. It keeps flowing.

Some people's paths end abruptly. Their disconnection from their physical bodies happens quickly, immediately. For other people, the journey will seem much slower. For example, there may be an illness that seems to take a toll on their bodies for many years. Or they may have been "slowing down" for a long time.

People who are goal-driven and focused on specific accomplishments in their lives may leave this life more suddenly than people who have spent many years primarily responding to their surrounding environments. Some people spend more of their lives in a less focused manner. They primarily observe and react to what is around them. They may have goals, but they are more likely to be general than specific. They want to enjoy life and they want to feel good, but they may not have strong purposes they are trying to accomplish to achieve those goals.

People who are oriented toward accomplishing certain tasks may leave more quickly when they have either accomplished those goals or have surrendered to the idea that they can not or will not complete them.

Dementia among people who have been connected to their physical bodies for many decades often occurs because they have a lot of resistance to the idea of leaving that physical perspective. They may have an erroneous sense of what death is. They may fear it. They may have come to believe some of the earthly-taught concepts: that their own existence ends with physical death, that they may face a judgment day, that they may be condemned into the human concept of hell. They may feel so connected to a person or place that they cannot imagine leaving, and they have forgotten that they will really not be leaving. Dementia allows the gradual eroding of resistance. People become less connected with their physical perspective and with this physical "reality."

One does not die in response to resistant thoughts overnight. Many are patterns that develop and last over extended periods of time, usually years. Don't be afraid of random thoughts – a thought you have for only a few moments is not going to "be the death of you."

There are many variables to the means of death. There is an old saying that we die the way we live. While there appear to be exceptions, we also have to keep in mind that we cannot know what was going on in the mind of another. We also can not know what was actually going on at the moment of death. What appears to us as a violent death may actually have been experienced as a peaceful transition. Why we die, and the method by which we make that change, are understood by us after it has happened – if we want to understand it. It may make no sense to us here on earth. In heaven, it will make sense, or we may be having such a good time we don't care!

«« Q »»
What is karma?

Karma is frequently misunderstood in terms of reciprocity that occurs from lifetime to lifetime. The idea is often discussed that if you do something bad to someone in this lifetime, something similar will happen to you in the next lifetime.

"Karma" is much more immediate than that. First of all, there are no "lessons" that we carry from one lifetime to another. We start fresh each time. There is no sense of punishment that if we do something wrong in this lifetime, the same thing is done to us in the next. This is a false belief.

Almost every religion and culture has some version of the principle that we call the Golden Rule: "Do unto others as you would have them do unto you."

Energetically, when I commit an act toward someone, I am emitting an energy field that matches what I am doing. The Universe matches my energy: like energies attract. So while I am emitting at this frequency, I am also attracting like energies. However I am treating other people, whatever I believe about other people: I am inviting the same back to me.

Let me offer an example. Let's say I am driving home from work and I need to stop at the grocery store. I am feeling rushed, feeling a shortage of time. So I cut someone off in the parking lot in order to get a closer parking space. Once in the store, I cut in front of someone who is heading to the cash register at the same time so I can check out first.

Then, on my way home, a car pulls in front of mine abruptly and cuts me off, slowing me down. The driver is clearly feeling the same way I am.

Like energies attract.

Instead of being mad at the driver, I would be wise to pay attention to what I am thinking and feeling and how I am treating others. When that driver cut me off, I lost the time I gained by being rude to others. If I had changed my energy at the beginning when I was feeling rushed and had not treated others disrespectfully, that driver would not have treated me the same way.

How you act and what you believe is reflected back to you. But the result is fairly immediate. If I change the energy I am emitting, then I change what I am attracting. The way others treat me is feedback about my own energy.

When we die, we are re-emerging into a loving, peaceful, joyful energy. We are returning home. When we come back to earth – when we assume a new body – we are coming from that place of love. What we are emitting energetically is love. We are not carrying forward any lessons from the past we "must" revisit. We are emitting love. Why do you think so many people find babies adorable? They are just arriving from the place we know as our loving home. They are reminding us, in their loving gaze, of the essence of life.

««« Q »»»
What are near-death experiences?

Near-death experiences are not the same as "death" experiences. Coming close to leaving your physical perspective is not the same as actually leaving it. But there are similarities.

When people have near-death experiences, they are entering a state of non-resistance. That means they are not having thoughts that are keeping them out of alignment with God or their God-self. They are in a place of allowing: allowing the love and well-being that flow to them all the time. Except, without resistant thoughts, they are actually *allowing* it. They can feel the fullness of who they really are.

In near-death experiences, if we have beliefs about what we will encounter when we die, we are likely to have exactly that experience. If we expect to appear at pearly gates, that is likely what we will see. If we expect to see God sitting on a throne of judgment, that is what we will see. We are in a state of non-resistance, but we are in a state of expectation. We have an expectation of what we will encounter when we die, and that is the experience we can manifest.

It is common for people to encounter loved ones who have already re-emerged. In reality, those loved ones are accessible to us while we are still in our physical bodies. But in a state of non-resistance, we now believe we can see them and communicate with them, so we allow it.

We have near-death experiences for many reasons. For some people, these experiences remove a fear of death. For others, it affirms for them the existence of God and Heaven. Some people find they return to their physical life on earth with more purpose and perhaps more urgency: they stop putting off what they have always wanted to do. Others retain the sense of connection and well-being they had in their experience. Some find that their priorities change:

what used to seem important and meaningful doesn't anymore. Every person has a unique perspective in near-death experiences; every person returns from it with a meaning unique to him or her.

The common threads in most near-death experiences are what we do encounter at death: feeling a rising, a re-emerging, a strong presence that we are loved and all is well. We see a brightness as we return to this higher energy, this higher frequency. We experience loved ones greeting us. We feel overwhelmingly loved and loving. There is an exhilaration, a depth of love and connection it can be difficult to describe from our physical perspective. Our sensory experience is sharpened, even though we are not seeing through physical eyes or hearing through physical ears anymore. Everything is vivid and wonderful. We can feel more alive in death than we have been feeling in life. We truly know and understand: *All is well.*

«« Q »»
Why did my loved one die so young?

It is a false belief that all of our spirits come into this world intending to live until our physical bodies are old. That is simply not the way the interplay of the spiritual and physical worlds works. Some people come in intending to live to be old. Some come in never intending to live in a physical body more than a few moments or years. It can seem hard to understand from our earthly perspective, but it is not difficult to comprehend from the non-physical perspective.

There are many, many reasons someone may choose to leave when the body is young. I could write a whole book discussing the possibilities and never come close to covering all of them. The reason your loved one left may not be known to you, or make sense to you, until *you* can also look at the situation from a non-physical perspective. You may be so focused on grief and loss that understanding will continue to elude you until you pass into the non-physical world yourself.

There are several points it might be helpful for you to understand.

Many spirits come into this world never intending to live a long physical life. So your loved one may never have intended to stay for a long time – even if that was what you wanted.

Your loved one may have come, at least in part, to help remind you (or others) of what is really important. Your loved one's death may have been part of an intention to return you – or other people – to a greater, more fulfilling life. Your loved one may have wanted to help you remember the eternal nature of life and love: that there is no death, that there is no end to love.

Your loved one may have found life in this physical realm to have been so difficult that returning to the non-physical realm seemed the easiest way to return quickly to a place of joy and happiness.

No one did anything wrong. If your loved one died at a time that the body was young, it was not senseless; there was a reason. There may have been another person or persons who played parts in your loved one making the transition to non-physical. You do not need to feel guilty. You have no reason to blame. There is nothing you should or could have done differently.

People do not die without reason. There is always a reason. We may not always be able to understand it, especially when we are grieving.

You will see and be with your loved one again. Your separation is only temporary.

If you want to communicate with your loved one, you can. But you need to move beyond your sadness and grief to make that possible. See the questions later in this book on communication with your loved one for more information about how you can allow that to happen. And yes, even if your loved one was an infant who never learned to speak, you can still communicate. Your earthly infant, in the non-physical realm, is a very wise being with fully developed communication skills. Your loved one may have been in the physical body of an infant, but the youth of the body does not reflect the maturity of the soul.

The reasons that people make their transitions to non-physical often have different layers. For instance, you may have seen a physical illness or "accident" take the life of your loved one. But the physical illness or accident may just have been the path of least resistance for your loved one to return to the non-physical world. There may have been other things going on that you were not aware of. Beyond what is happening on this physical plane are the happenings in the non-physical realm.

For instance, maybe your loved one wanted to make a new entrance as a physical being, and the people that he or she wanted to be born to were about to have a baby. There was an opening in the non-physical world, an opportunity that you would not have been aware of. For example, maybe your husband wanted to grow up to be your newborn son's best friend rather than his father. So he is born somewhere else to people you don't know, but meets your son later in life and the two have an incredible bond that serves them both very well. You meet this young man later and feel a strong connection to him; you really like him, even though you don't understand why. There are endless possibilities.

We stay connected to each other through many lifetimes. We come into physical experiences together, or we find each other once we are here. There is really no end to the possibilities.

I know it is hard not to think of your loved one's death as a tragedy. But try to focus instead on the myriad of new opportunities available to your loved one. Your loved one is happy. And remember: you will be together again.

««« Q »»»
How is the soul affected if the body is cremated?

When a person dies, their spirit immediately exits the connection with the physical body. The departure is instant and complete. Once a person has left, anything that is done to the body will not affect the spirit.

It does not matter if the body is cremated. It does not matter how long the body is kept around until it is buried, whether that time is short or long.

It does not matter if the body, or cremains (ashes), are moved. It does not matter if the body, in whatever form, is moved repeatedly after death.

The peace and joy of the spirit are in no way dependent on a peaceful resting place for the body or ashes of the body. A person's spirit is not affected by any acts that seem, to us, to dishonor or desecrate the body.

Sometimes, people don't follow their loved one's wishes for the disposition of his or her body. Your loved ones in non-physical understand this, even if they did not when they were living on earth. They don't harbor resentments, or feel that you broke a promise.

It also does not bother them in heaven if their body is missing and not recovered, or has been disposed of without the ceremony of their chosen religious tradition.

They have moved on and are giving their attention to other things. If you have not yet, they are urging you to move forward with your life as well.

The fullness of love and joy the spirit is experiencing in its fuller connection with God so dominates the well-being of the soul that nothing can diminish it. Nothing.

«« Q »»
My loved one died alone and I feel very guilty about it.

Actually, your loved one didn't die alone. No one "dies" alone.

You may not have been physically present with your loved one's physical body when your loved one made a return to the non-physical realm. But there were many other spirits there: spirits who love this person. As we prepare to make our transition, we can become much more attune to the non-physical world.

Think of the stories you have heard of people who, shortly before they died, made reference to people who had passed on before them as if they were in the room together or they were conversing in the present moment. If no one else in that room saw or heard the other voice or spirit, it is because no one else in the room was attuned to the non-physical realm the way that dying person was.

People in the non-physical realm get excited when someone they love is going to re-emerge into non-physical and they will get to spend time together again. Think about waiting a long time to see someone you really love. If you heard they were about to arrive for a visit, wouldn't you be there to greet them? Think about the wonderful time your loved one is going to have after making that transition.

When you re-emerge into heaven, you see people in the non-physical from other lifetimes you have had, too. So if a person lived a short or solitary life this time, there are still many loving people in heaven from other lifetimes.

Making the transition is not difficult the way it is when we come into an earthly body. People don't need help to make the transition into non-physical. We have all done it many times before. But sometimes we need help letting go of the focus on the physical realm. Sometimes we need a little encouragement to let go, or some reassurance that it will be okay when we "die" simply because we have forgotten.

No one, absolutely no one, dies alone. You have nothing to worry about or feel guilty for. Your loved one doesn't blame you or feel like you did anything wrong. Forgive yourself; there really is nothing to forgive.

«« Q »»
I never got to say good-bye to my loved one.

First of all, you can still say good-bye. Communication with your loved one in the non-physical world is just as easy as it would have been here – even more so. If you didn't say good-bye in this realm, or didn't tell the person how much you loved him or her, just start thinking about your loved one and tell your loved one now what you want to say. Your loved one may already know this, if you've been thinking it or feeling it. But you can also say it to your loved one now. It is not too late. It is never too late.

Second, any good-bye is only a temporary good-bye. You will see your loved one again. You will be together again. It will happen. So realize that the separation between the two of you is temporary.

Third, the separation between the physical and non-physical worlds is an illusion. It is not real. It is what we have been taught and what we have come to believe but it is not correct. So you can continue to communicate with your loved one when you want to and are in a place where you are feeling really good and happy.

Have you ever heard children who talked to people that seemed to you imaginary? Have you ever known animals who "saw" things in a room that you didn't see? As adults, we have trained ourselves out of communicating with the non-physical world. Children are born knowing how to do this. Animals know how to do this.

We train this ability out of our children. We tell them that their invisible friend is something they made up and isn't real. We teach them that these communications are impossible. We laugh at people who profess the ability to communicate with "the dead" or spirits. We ridicule children who talk to spirits that we can't see. Our message to children is that if you want to be accepted in our society, you must conform to our social standards – and we don't consider it "acceptable" to talk to the dead. We don't consider it acceptable to talk *about* the dead in the present tense – because they are still alive, they just aren't in physical bodies anymore.

Children who talk with their loved ones on the other side tend to be much happier and healthier because they know there is no such thing as "dead." Children who remember people and experiences they had from the non-physical realm or other lives approach this life from a fuller, happier, more holistic perspective.

Ironically, we are trying to learn today what we were already born knowing, and had to unlearn to fit into "normal" society.

Your loved one still lives, and you can still communicate.

«« Q »»
I have received a terminal diagnosis, and I am really scared.
I don't want my life to end.

First, there is no end to you. You are an eternal being. So do not think of this diagnosis as indicating an end to you or to your relationships with the people you love. The relationships with the people you love are eternal, just like you are.

Second, medical diagnoses are like photographs: they show one moment in time. Many people have received terminal diagnoses and gone on to live long lives. Many others have not. If you fully believe what the doctors tell you, then you may be agreeing to end this physical expression of your life on their terms. That's okay, if that's what you choose. But I encourage you to express your life on your terms. As much as you can, continue to focus on aspects of life that make you happy, that give you pleasure, that please you. Become selfish in finding joy. Make being joyful really important to you.

Third, think of a "terminal" diagnosis in terms of the word. A terminal is a place you go when you are traveling – like a train station or a plane "terminal" on the way to your next destination. It is not about an end – not at all. It is an indicator that you are traveling. It is about movement – not about endedness.

You are on a journey. That's what this diagnosis means. You may not know yet where this journey takes you, in the short run. In the long run, we are all going to leave the perspective of our bodies some day and return to heaven, return to the non-physical home we came from. In that sense, our lives here are always temporary. They always have a beginning and an end, in a very concrete sense, through the expression of our physical bodies. But – and this is a big *but* – the terminal diagnosis you received may have simply reminded you of this. It may have reminded

63

you of the fact that you are on a journey. You may have been expecting to live many more years in the same place you are right now. But you are a traveler.

Many people who receive terminal diagnoses feel like it is a wake-up call. They were not living their lives fully, joyfully. They were spending a lot of time focusing on things that did not please them, that did not feel good to think about. The diagnosis caused them to look differently at the world and the people around them. They began spending more time pursuing what they wanted in life. Projects that had been moved to the back burner – that long list of things you always wanted to get around to "someday"– can be given a new priority in your life. Start living. If you have a list of things you want to do before you "kick the bucket" then now is the time to start experiencing them.

If you don't get them all done in this life, you can continue to get them done in your next life or after you have left your present perspective. You will be back on earth again, with the people you love, in a life of new creation. This diagnosis is more about the act of the play changing than the play ending.

A diagnosis is just an indicator. Let it be a wake-up call to a new beginning, not an alarm going off about an ending. You are going to continue to live, whether it is in this body or not. You are going to continue to travel to new places. You will also continue to be with the people you love, just maybe not in your current body at this particular destination. When you go somewhere on a short trip, you say goodbye to your family expecting to be back home soon, seeing them again. That expectation does not need to change. You will see them again and be with them again. This is a short-term change. In the long-view of eternity, what appears to you like an impending separation will seem momentary.

This life has always been just one stop on a never-ending trip. Your "diagnosis" has just made you more aware of it. Continue to live your life on earth as happily and as fully as you can while you are here. Enjoy this destination, but don't be anxious about the next one. You may not know it yet, but you will be happy there.

««« Q »»»

I always wanted my father to be at my wedding. But he died two years ago. I so wish he could see it. My wedding day just won't be the same without him.

People often talk about their "dead" loved ones missing the celebrations and accomplishments of their lives. But you need to realize that your loved ones still attend these events, and still have knowledge of what is going on.

It is very likely, even probable, that your father will be at your wedding. Do you really think he would miss an occasion so important to you both? Just because he will not be there in a physical body does not mean that he will not be present. He will be there, and will be enjoying it every bit as much as you hoped he would.

You can internally acknowledge your loved ones at these occasions. They can receive your thoughts and know you are thinking about them. You can also honor them in other, more visible ways if you choose.

The spirits of our loved ones are still alive. They still love and care about us, just as we do about them. They continue to maintain an interest in our lives. They join us for those special occasions that are meaningful to us and to them. They see the children and grandchildren born. They watch them grow up. They attend weddings and graduations. You want your father to be at your wedding; your father wants to be there, too. I doubt there is any way he would miss it.

«« Q »»
*When I was a soldier in Iraq during the war, one of my
buddies was killed during a mortar attack. I was only injured.
I feel terribly guilty, like it should have been me who died.
Why was it him and not me?*

I know it is hard to get away from the concept that
death is a bad thing. You may have been taught that for
many years. But your friend is fine now. Your friend is
happy now. You may miss your friend, but you don't need to
feel guilty about the fact that he is dead. The spirit of your
friend, which you came to know through his physical body,
is still very much alive. You don't need to feel badly for him.
And you definitely don't need to feel guilty that you still
have the perspective of a physical body.

Just because someone's physical body is no longer
inhabitable does not mean his spirit "dies." We simply leave
our bodies when they are no longer inhabitable. The body
has served its purpose.

The question of why him and not you is a different one.

We cannot know what was going on for him at a non-
physical level. We don't know what communication he was
having with his God-self. We don't know what decisions he
was making at a broader, non-physical level, or what issues
he was dealing with.

People in these situations often have a sense that their
physical experience will be concluding soon. We often refer
to this as intuition, gut instinct, or premonition.

Sometimes, this is a way of helping people prepare for
death. If they listen to their intuition, they can tend to details
that may be helpful to those around them when they die.
They may still make plans for the future. But they may also
take action that will help them to "wrap up" this physical
experience.

The means by which we "die" is usually the path of least resistance. It is the easiest path available to us to re-emerge back into the non-physical realm, or heaven.

Sometimes, we decide it is time to go, and we simply go home.

Other times, we are resisting the call forward into a fuller existence. We want to be happy, but we keep fighting our own movement forward. Our desire to be happy gets greater, and our resistance to moving toward that happiness also gets greater.

In these kinds of circumstances, we get indicators. Our God-self calls us forward, and we don't go. Our God-self calls us forward and calls us forward and calls us forward but we stubbornly choose to stay where we are miserable. Repeatedly. The strong negative emotions we are feeling are clear indicators that we are not following our own path to bliss. We created the path ourselves, but we're stubbornly insisting on staying right where we are.

So then we get physical warnings. For instance, people who are killed in car accidents often get earlier "warnings." Sometimes minor car accidents, just as an example, precede major accidents. Someone has lesser falls before having a major fall.

You have to remember that we are like radio stations that are transmitting energy. We are transmitting all the time.

We are also receiving – we receive energy back on the same frequency we are broadcasting.

So what is going on in our lives tells us, not just what we are receiving, but what we are transmitting. We receive and transmit on the same frequency.

If you don't like what is happening in your life, you need to adjust the frequency of what you are transmitting. You need to change your energy. And the wonderful part is: you have the power to do that. In fact, you are the only person with the power to do that. No one else can transmit or receive energy for you.

People who are "killed" like your friend are making a quick transition back to the non-physical realm. This may have been the easiest path for your friend to get quickly to a place of great joy. It may be that he was on a frequency of vulnerability where he had earlier signs that something was out of alignment, indicating to him that he needed to change his energetic "frequency." He may have been given a "gut feeling" by his God-self to move out of the way of the mortar that day and he didn't listen for some reason. These are things we simply don't know.

What we do know is that your friend is now in a place of great joy. He is available to communicate with you, if you want to talk with him. You don't need to be sorry he is dead. He is happy. He will come back into this physical realm when he is ready to. One physical existence is over for him, yes. But there is no end to him. This is what is most important for you to understand.

Ask him for a sign that he is okay. When he gives it to you, if you are open to seeing it, then you will realize he is still very much "alive."

«« Q »»

When I was in the military, we were at war and I was put in situations where I had to kill people. It was them or me. And it haunts me now. I was told there was a difference between killing and murdering, that murdering was personal and killing was something you did because it was your job. They said that's why killing in war isn't in violation of the Ten Commandments: it's not the same as murder. Regardless of the rationalization, I can't let go of what I did. The images, the sounds, the smells, the tastes: they still haunt me. They were people. And I killed them.

There is no easy way to answer this question. What you experienced was horrible. There is no getting around that. What is most important now is that you come to terms with it so that you can let it go. You need to let the past be the past. As long as you keep focusing on your memories of it, it will continue to become the present. Again and again. And if you start to anticipate, and have anxiety, about intrusive memories reasserting themselves in your experience, the past becomes the future. You need to stop that from happening.

You are the only one who can control that. You are the only one who can let the past go. You are in control of your thoughts, even if it doesn't always feel that way.

You need to know that the people you killed have forgiven you. If they did not do it when they were alive, they did it after they were dead. Once they were dead, they understood. They saw the entire experience from a broader perspective. They do not blame you for what happened.

It sounds like you are having a difficult time forgiving yourself. If the people you killed have forgiven you, then doesn't it make sense that you need to let it go, too?

The people who died are in heaven. They are in a much happier place now than where they were before. You, focusing on the horror of their death, does not serve them. It does not serve you, either.

Let yourself move into love. I know that sounds like a huge stretch from where you are right now. But let love be your new focus. The people who, in your images are dead or dying, are still very much alive – and in a place of great love. They are feeling loved, and they feel love for you. You can feel love for them and rejoice for them. You can feel love for yourself and let go of the past. Because it is, truly, past. It is no longer your experience or theirs. It is over. Let it be over. Let the past be the past.

You can get to love gradually. Start by being kinder to yourself. You have been very hard on yourself. Very hard.

You need to create new images to focus on when, and if, you start to feel the old memories intruding. Make time to generate intentionally a list of positive memories. If none come to mind, ask your friends or family for times they remember you being happy. If you still can't retrieve any, then intentionally set about to *make* some positive memories. You can create them now.

Spend time with each of these good memories. Let the experiences become vivid. Try to make each one alive with sensory memories. Remember the sensations, sights, sounds, smells, tastes you associate with each positive memory.

Keep this list of good memories where you can easily find it. You might even want to make copies to keep in your wallet, at home, at work, in your vehicle. You could record yourself talking about a good memory and save it to your cell phone, so you can remind yourself anytime you need it. Save it on your computer. Make your good memories as accessible as possible.

Surround yourself with good-feeling thoughts. Put up photographs or other items that remind you of good times.

You learned strong discipline in the military. It is time to apply that sense of discipline to your thoughts. You *can*

71

control your thoughts. You must. Be gentle with yourself as you practice. Over time, you will get more experienced, and it will become easier.

Do not expect just to *stop* these thoughts. You need to replace bad memories with good memories. You need to replace painful thoughts with happier ones. *You can do it.*

Another technique you might find helpful is that, if images of people you killed come to mind, *re-imagine* them. Tune in to where the souls of these people are *now*, not at the moment of their physical deaths. You aren't there any more; don't require them to be. Take them – and you – out of the tortured experience of war. Create new, joyful settings in your mind. This is where these souls are now. Let those images replace the ones that are haunting you. When you start to have an old image, stop it and replace it with this new one. Those people are happy now and they want you to be, too. You are not dishonoring them – or you – by focusing on the present instead of the past.

Work on finding happiness. Make that your quest. Work on finding thoughts that feel better to you, that feel good. It is okay to let go of the past; in fact, you must. And, with time, practice, patience, and kindness to yourself, you will.

«« Q »»

My daughter committed suicide while she was away at college. How can I ever know the reason why? Her friends could only speculate.

I know this will be hard to hear, but the reason your daughter committed suicide is not important now. Part of the reason you want to know is to understand if you did something wrong, or someone else did, or if there is a way you could have prevented it. You want to blame someone; in fact, you are blaming yourself already. That is natural for a parent in our society to do. But the reason she decided to exit from this physical existence is not really important now.

What is important for you to understand is that your daughter is happy now. Yes, she was unhappy enough, and felt trapped enough, that the only solution she saw to her problem was to end this physical existence. But your daughter still lives. Her spirit is alive and free and joyful. She is living, in the non-physical world, the best existence you could imagine for her. You always wanted her to be happy. Now she is.

It is interesting that your daughter was able to stay enough in touch with her God-self that she remembered what death really is. It was not only that she wanted to end her own suffering. She knew, really *knew*, that she would find peace and relief and joy in the state that we call death. She knew this. She did not doubt this. She knew she would feel fulfilled there.

She also knew that she would see you again. She did not feel like she was ending her relationship with you because she was ending the life of her physical body. Again, she was in touch enough with the God-self part of her to know that her love for you would continue. Your relationship has not ended. It will continue. For a while – a long while, you will continue to have the perspective of a physical body and she will have the perspective of non-physical. But there is nothing for you to feel guilty about. You did not do anything wrong.

Try to keep your focus not on the physical lack of her in your existence now, but on the joy she is currently feeling. You can still talk to her. She wants to communicate with you, from her perspective in the non-physical world. And if you do start to find her around you, you will find relief in the knowledge that she is an eternal being: a joyful eternal being. You will be together again. The physical separation is only temporary.

«« Q »»

I am a medical professional and work in a hospital. It is always hard when a patient dies. But it is especially hard when children die. I always feel like we should have been able to do something to save them. The deaths of infants, in particular, really haunt me. How can I cope with this better? It is really tearing me apart.

The first thing I would advise you to do is to keep your focus on where the soul of that child is now. The soul of that child is happy, free, enjoying a different kind of life than in an earthly body. But that child is still very much alive.

Most people who have trouble with death focus on the idea that death is an end. Yes, a child's death marks the end of a dream for parents who envisioned that child growing into adulthood. But it is not the end of the child. It is not even the end of that child's relationship with his or her parents. Those relationships are eternal. They will continue to be together at another time.

Not all children are born with a plan or intent to live into adulthood. Some children come forth only intending to live a brief existence. Some would prefer an intense, brief life on earth to a prolonged one.

It is important to try to see the situation the way God does.

God does not see something gone terribly wrong when a child, even an infant, dies. God knows they are eternal beings. God knows they live on. They have had a short time to have that particular earthly perspective. But this child still lives. This child will have other earthly experiences, other earthly perspectives. This was not the child's first earthly existence, and will certainly not be the child's last. God stays focused on the bigger picture.

We usually make our exit from this earthly life through the path of least resistance. Sometimes the path of least resistance is through an illness or accident. This may be of little comfort in the moment. But what you are seeing manifest in the child's body is that path of least resistance.

When anyone is sick and suffering in his or her physical body, the sense of relief which is felt at the moment of death is huge. To go from a place where one feels trapped in one's body, in physical pain or discomfort, to a place of freedom, great love, and joy: the contrast is immense.

Given your profession, you will always be dealing with people in grief when a loved one dies. But keep your focus on where the soul of that child is now, on the love and joy that child is feeling. The child's family may not be able to find comfort in that, but you can. It may take work to learn this new perspective. You will need to practice it. Try to see the situation, and the spirit of that child, the way God does. And you can hopefully find enough peace to continue in the profession you have chosen.

«« Q »»
*My nephew was killed in a car accident. I spoke to a medium
after his death, and he told her he had not intended to die so
young. How could this be possible?*

Usually, when someone is killed in a car accident or
other tragedy, there have been advance indicators. For
instance, many of the people killed in the 9/11 tragedy had
some pre-knowledge that they might die soon. The larger
part of them, their God-selves, knew what was coming, and
helped them to prepare. They may have had feelings that
something significant would happen soon, or even that their
physical lives would end.

At other times, people get warnings about the direction
their lives are heading. For instance, the adults I have
known who were killed in car accidents often had caution
signs. They were experiencing strong negative feelings
about an aspect of their lives; an aspect might have been
deemed in crisis. Or they had experiences which could have
been interpreted as warning bells before the larger
accident. Some had smaller accidents. Some tended to get
distracted and lose focus, and didn't pay enough attention
to the present moment. There were smaller incidents, like
falling off a ladder, tripping and injuring themselves, or
closely avoiding a serious accident, that could have been
indicators to them to stop and assess what was going on.

Sometimes, people may have strong gut instincts or
intuitive feelings but override them. For instance, someone
might have a strong feeling that he shouldn't get into a car
when a friend who has drunk too much is driving. But he
doesn't want to offend his friend, so he gets in anyway.
Their God-self is offering them guidance, but they are
choosing not to listen. A woman might feel strongly she
shouldn't get on a plane, but doesn't want to have to explain
to her companions why she wants to take a later flight.
Intuition and gut instinct are greatly respected by some in

77

this society, but trivialized by others. This is guidance from your God-self, and it is important to listen.

Some people like to take risks. They feel immortal. They forget they are in a physical body. And some of these people would rather live dangerously and risk dying young than live safely and more moderately for a longer time.

It may not be that your nephew had intended to die then, or that way. But I would suspect he had guidance that, once he was in non-physical, he was able to interpret. He had an "Aha!" moment, and wishes now he had listened to the guidance he received when he was still in a physical body.

Tragic accidents are not simply accidental. They don't happen "out of the blue" for no reason at all. Our God-selves are always there guiding us, but we have to be open and listen. Often, we tune that part of ourselves out.

You cannot know what was going on with your nephew. You can not know his internal thoughts and struggles. I have known many people who seemed happy, but weren't. They presented one face to the world, and kept the darker part of themselves private.

If you establish communication with your nephew, you might ask him what indicators he had that he was out-of-alignment with his larger intention to live a longer physical life. Had he been offered guidance that he needed to slow down and honor the fact he was having a physical experience? Had other events indicated to him that we was not paying enough attention to the present moment? Were there thoughts or anxieties that had worried and distracted him? Was he unhappy? Did he simply override strong non-physical guidance? Did he have moments where he simply tuned out the physical world around him? There can be many reasons for the accident. And it may not have been his conscious intention. But his non-physical self, his God-self, could see it coming. If it was not deemed to be in his best interest, then he was warned. But our God-selves cannot override our free will to make the choices we do. They guide us to better choices, but we still have to listen. How many times in our lives have we said something like, "I had a feeling I shouldn't" or "I knew better" – after the fact? Hindsight is clearer and your nephew has that now. Divine guidance is always available, but we still have to listen and follow it.

«« Q »»

My baby simply died in her sleep one night. She appeared perfect; there was nothing wrong with her. I can't get over the feeling that I did something terribly wrong. If I had only woken up sooner, she might still be alive. How could that have happened?

What happens when infants die in their sleep this way is similar to what is happening with miscarriages. There is simply a change in intention from the non-physical level. No one did anything wrong. It was not that you did not love her enough or make her happy enough. Waking up sooner would not have changed anything.

These kinds of deaths can be very challenging to understand from our human perspective. We think there must have been something wrong. Perhaps we did something wrong. We blame ourselves. How could such a perfect gift have been taken away from us so quickly?

From the non-physical level, the view is quite different. First, the relationship you have with your daughter is eternal. It is not limited to this physical experience. You have already been together for many lifetimes, and you will be together again for many more. This relationship has not ended. The two of you are simply not going to have a physical experience together right now.

Second, again from the non-physical level, nothing has gone wrong. When you are looking at the situation from a broader view, you see a bigger picture. I know this can be hard to understand. But the intentions of many people and many decades of time are being considered. There has simply been a change in thought: not right now.

Third, usually when an infant is not born or dies young, the infant re-emerges back into a physical body later in the same family. If you give birth to another baby, you may find that she returns to you – in a girl's or boy's body. The gender may change, even if it is the same soul. She may return as your son or daughter. She may be your granddaughter. She may be your niece. Do not assume it is the same soul, but trust your intuition and internal guidance if she feels the same to you. Also realize that her role in that life, whatever it is, is in that new relationship to you and not this old role she has left.

Your daughter did not choose to leave from a physical level. She did not make a conscious decision that something was wrong and it was time to depart. These kinds of decisions are made at the non-physical level.

Women who have miscarriages may be undergoing the same process. There was a decision made at the non-physical level not to come forward right now. There has been a change of intention. That's all.

We see death as a bad thing. From the non-physical level, it is not. From the non-physical level, the relationship continues. It is more like deciding: I am going to play a different role in this drama. Or I am going to change the movie I was going to see. These changes are not seen as tragedies from the non-physical level.

These kinds of deaths can present great opportunities. Your daughter is alive and wants to communicate with you. She wants you to know she is all right. She wants you to know you did nothing wrong. She wants you to know that your own God-self, from the non-physical perspective, knows that events will eventually unfold so you are reunited, even happier together, sharing a greater bond with one another.

This relationship has not ended. It will continue. Your love for each other has not ended. There is no end to eternal love.

This re-emergence has provided you with an opportunity to understand there is much more to life than you see and know from your physical perspective. There is a much bigger, broader picture. There is more to your relationships than you experience here on earth.

You have an opportunity to expand your understanding of life and death. You can come to learn about death from a new perspective. You can appreciate that she is not dead, she is not ended. She is still very much alive. You may eventually find you can lose your own fear of death, and be of comfort to others in similar experiences.

Your daughter will continue to be with you and around you. She says it is her turn to watch over you now. She loves you always.

«« Q »»

I read that the souls of children who die very young have to be tended in heaven by their relatives. What if children don't have relatives in heaven to take care of them?

First, let's revisit the concept of soul. Just because someone is in a young body here on earth does not mean that the soul is young. In fact, the soul is not young.

Many of us have met a child whose relatives commented, "That child has a very 'old' soul." It means that child seems wise beyond the number of physical years spent here on earth.

Souls come into infant bodies because that is how the spirits of people re-emerge into the physical experience. There is a very different vibrational energy in the non-physical world than there is here on earth. Spirits need time to adjust their energy patterns to our earthly energy patterns. That is partially what "growing up" on earth is about.

Have you ever noticed how much more easily most children seem to heal from a physical illness than we do? As "older" adults who have been kicking around here on earth for a while, most of us have developed beliefs and energy patterns that are further away from our God-self than young children. When children get sick while they are young, they can get very sick because the earthly vibration can be much lower than their souls in the non-physical world. But it is that same connection that allows them to be so loving and resilient. They can usually recover faster than adults. Once they have retuned the frequency of their vibration to who they really are, it is easier for them to align with it.

As we get older, we often get further away from that original God-self frequency. We forget what it is, and we forget how to realign with it. We become more concerned with what others think of us, and give the earthly perspectives of others more weight than the God-self frequency within us. Kids can tune in faster to who they really are. When they tune out, it may be a dramatic tuning out. But it can also be easier for them to retune vibrationally.

When children die – when their spirit leaves the perspective of the physical body and returns to reunite with the God perspective – they are instantly fully whole again. They are joyful and happy and experience the full wisdom of their wise expanded selves. They have full access to the wisdom of God – to the wisdom that has created universes. They don't need anyone to take care of them. They are not "young" and inexperienced in heaven. They are wise and powerful. They are love in its deepest and fullest sense. The physical body was young in earthly terms, but the soul is wise, eternal and timeless.

I must note here, for those of you who have had a beloved child die, that your child is still with you. That spirit still comes and visits you. If you like, you can talk with your child. And while you may recognize the spirit of your child, that spirit will also seem wise beyond the years you knew that child lived here on earth. Remember: you and your child will be reunited again. The "separation" you experience is temporary.

It is important to remember that the spirit of your child cannot reconnect with you here if you continue to grieve. Your grief takes you so far away from the joyful and loving experience your child is having that your child cannot reach you. The frequency of where you are, in grief, is distant from the frequency where your child is. If you stay in pain, you cannot reconnect with your child while you are still here on earth. Focus on the love you experienced with that child, focus on the happy memories, and allow yourself to be joyful for the happiness your child has now. That will move you closer to where your child presently is. Remember: your child knows you will be together again, and that you can still connect now. You are experiencing a separation that your child is not. If you stay in your grief, you are choosing to stay apart from your child. Find joy and find your child.

««« Q »»»
I heard that sometimes, when people die, their souls get trapped here on earth and that's what creates a ghost.
Is there a difference between ghosts and spirits?

Ghosts and spirits are two different things. A spirit is the soul, the eternal non-physical energy that comes forth into the physical body to have an experience on earth. When a person dies, that energy leaves the physical body and returns to heaven, to the non-physical world.

Ghosts are residual energies. For instance, in a house that might be considered haunted, you may see a ghost image of a person walking through a certain room. This image may be seen by people for hundreds of years. Sometimes, something traumatic happened suddenly to create a very strong impression of energy. Other times, someone created a strong pattern of energy from doing the same action over and over – walking up and down a hallway while worrying about an ill child or spouse, for instance. The ghost is the residual energy that still exists from those actions.

Energy is a living thing. While ghosts do not have a soul, the ghost energy has an imprint of a spirit from the person or animal that it originated from. You may observe a ghost energy. Or people who are sensitive to these types of energy may be able to tune into the thoughts and feelings that person was having, that helped to create the energetic impression.

A person who is clairvoyant may be able to tune into the souls of people who are now in the non-physical realm, as well as the ghost energies of people. Those beings, in non-physical, could tell you how they died, but they would not have negative emotion about the death. They are in a state of joy now. If a clairvoyant tunes into the ghost energy of a person's traumatic death, you might learn details about what the person was feeling and experiencing. Since the person's soul is no longer experiencing that, there is really no need for you to, either.

The other important aspect to remember in those cases is that you might get details about the death of someone's body as those details are being interpreted through our physical experience. But as someone dies, he or she is often experiencing a kind of ease that we can't interpret in the physical world. So the death might seem much longer and worse to you than that individual actually experienced. And it would certainly seem far worse to you now, since you are still in the physical realm and probably missing that person, than it does to the one who has moved into heaven, far beyond it. The soul of someone who is undergoing a traumatic death often removes itself from the trauma before it happens, or as it begins to happen. If you imagine the traumatic death of a loved one, you are imagining the person fully present for the experience. That is not necessarily what happened.

The soul and God-self help to protect an individual from trauma. Because the body was still alive does not mean the soul was still present. Being physically alive does not always mean that the soul is still attached. Bodies can continue to live even when the soul has left.

I have spoken to adults who had traumatic experiences as children. Many of these adults shared how they felt like they were observing these traumas: they were floating above the body watching what was happening. They did not return to the body until the trauma was over. If one is watching a trauma and then the body dies, the soul has no need to return to the body. It simply re-emerges back into the non-physical realm.

A God who loves unconditionally would never condemn someone's soul to be trapped and bound to earth at death. The soul always returns, immediately, to the non-physical realm. But because people have not understood energy, they have confused the soul with energetic residue. No one is trapped on earth at death. But there can be residual energy. The energy will eventually dissipate. But as people see it and give their attention to it, they are contributing energy to its continued existence.

In order to "see a ghost," people usually have to be in the same emotional range as the residual energy. If I am happy most of the time, I am not likely to encounter a suffering ghost. People who are fearful or feel vulnerable to these types of energies are most likely to encounter them. You have to be on a similar frequency to pick up the energy.

If you worry your home is haunted, try to make peace with the energy that is there. When you are giving it your attention, you are activating it more: stirring it up, so to speak. If you are happy and living a joyful life, a lower frequency energy will simply leave. Activate what feels good to you, not what worries you. Engage in activities that help you feel strong, not vulnerable.

Have you ever noticed how someone can live in a home that others consider haunted, but they are not bothered by it? They may or may not recognize that "weird" things go on sometimes...but it doesn't bother them. They choose to direct their attention elsewhere. They are not a match to any unhappy residual energy.

What often is not discussed is that there can be happy residual energy. Have you ever walked into a room after something wonderful happened there, and it just felt good? Go somewhere after a really joyful celebration and soak it in. Homes where a happy family or loving couple lived for years can feel really wonderful.

The full range of energetic frequencies is always available. You get to choose which frequency you tune to.

«« Q »»
I am so mad at God. Why did God let this happen?

You may be angry at God for the death of a loved one, or for your own impending death. You may be mad because you are going to die sooner that you wanted, or because you think God "took" your loved one too early. There are many reasons you might be angry with God. And that's okay. God doesn't mind. God can take it.

First of all, being angry with God can be a step forward in your healing, in your accepting whatever the situation is that you feel you have no control over. Feeling angry feels better than feeling helpless, powerless, weak, or depressed. Feeling angry feels better than immense pain or grief. It feels better than sadness. Being angry can be a part of the grieving process. And it can help move you in the right direction. It is okay to be angry. Don't get mad at yourself for being angry. Don't let other people shut your anger down because they are uncomfortable with it.

It's okay to be angry right now. You won't stay angry forever. Don't take action from a place of anger. But let yourself have the feelings.

God is glad you're angry. What?! Really? Yes, God is glad you are angry, because it means you are moving back into a place of empowerment. You are heading in the right direction. God wants you to feel better. And feeling angry right now, for a little while, means you are working into a place where you will feel better.

Why did God let this happen? Why did God end this physical life so soon? These are questions you may not want my answers to yet. So don't read the rest of this section until you are ready to hear those answers.

God did not make this happen. God did not choose to end this life. These ideas come from a false concept of who God is. Yes, God is the most powerful force in the universe, in all the universes. But God is a loving force. God is a loving being. God did not choose to bring you grief.

There are two important ideas to understand here.

First, God does not see death as bad because God knows that you and your loved ones are eternal beings. God knows that when people on earth die, they are just leaving their bodies and their earthly perspectives. They are returning to a place where they will feel more love and feel closer to God. God knows you will all be together again. God knows your separation is only temporary. So death is not a big deal to God the way it is to us. Because God understands. God doesn't have the misconceptions of death that we do. When you truly understand what we call earthly "death" then it is not as big a deal as we humans make it. Because there is no death. There is a recycling of the body and a renewed perspective. But the soul never ends. You and your loved ones never end. That is a false concept.

Second, God did not decide to "take" someone's life. God did not decide it was time for you or your loved one to die. God doesn't make those decisions.

The concept of a judgmental God is thousands of years old, when people believed in the existence of multiple gods and goddesses ruling our planet and the heavens. They believed that the gods and goddesses were in control of everything. When we read stories today, for example, of Greek and Roman mythology, they are "stories" to us. But ancient peoples used to believe these stories. When humans were introduced to the idea of one god instead of many, they folded in their centuries-old beliefs of many gods. This one God would embody the qualities of the many. God was all-powerful, but also all-controlling, judgmental, vengeful – representing both the best and the worst of human behavior. The "radical" concept of a single god like Jesus taught was presented to bridge what people then believed with the new direction that spiritual teachers were leading.

Ancient peoples believed the gods were in control of everything: they controlled the seasons, the weather, the stars, and determined what was "good" and "bad" and who lived and died.

But our God does not. The old beliefs were based on superstition. People were attempting to gain some control, some understanding of why events happened the way they did.

God does not control our lives. God does not try to teach us lessons. God does not judge us. God does not issue death sentences. God loves us. God loves us. God loves us.

We have free will. It is not conditional free will. God does not say, you have free will unless you mess up your life, and then I will take free will away from you.

You may not understand why your loved one died, or why you die, until you are back in the non-physical world. But then you will be able to understand if you want to. It will make sense to you then.

The "whys" you are asking may not be able to be answered while you are here on earth. Even if your questions are answered, you need to be in a place where you are open to receiving and are listening for an answer.

Some people only come to earth to stay for a little while. Some plan to be born and then decide not to be. Some of us want to live forever and don't understand the value of returning to non-physical for a fresh perspective. There are so many reasons, so many possibilities.

What you do need to understand is that God loves you. If you get angry with God, that's okay: you are doing nothing wrong by being angry. You will see your loved ones again. Your loved ones that have returned to non-physical are happy. You will be, too, when you get there. And God loves you, no matter what you do or how you feel. God loves you.

We adopted a child a few years ago. This child is so much like my mother that sometimes I think I am looking at my mother in her childhood all over again. But how could that be? Could this be my mother? This child was born in a different country to people I never met. Wouldn't she have been born to someone in our family if she were my mother?

The Universe is an amazing place. Yes, this could be the soul of your mother re-emerged into the body of this child. If your mother wanted to come back to you, and you wanted to welcome her back into your lives, then the Universe could easily have accommodated your intentions. In the grand scheme of things, the situation you describe is not so remarkable. These kinds of events, that seem to us to be miracles, happen all the time.

First of all, remember that relationships with our loved ones are eternal, as long as we want them to be. Yes, we do often come back to earth and "play" with each other here in the physical realm just as we "play" together in the non-physical realm. Creating different lives together can be a lot of fun, and very rewarding.

Second, the Universe orchestrates events all the time that unfold in what seem amazing ways. But this is the way God works. I am always surprised at how much I continue to be surprised! Once you understand these kinds of events are possible and happen all the time, it still seems imcredible.

You need to recognize that the spirit in your now-daughter's body is going to grow up as your daughter. She does not remember the life she had as your mother. There may be times she gets glimpses of it. If she tells you that you used to be *her* daughter, it is certainly okay to acknowledge it. You might say something like, "Yes, I was your daughter, and now you're my daughter. Isn't life great?" Providing her with an acceptance that her knowing is accurate will be helpful to her.

But it is also up to you to realize that this child is not your mother, in the sense that she is not here in this physical life to be motherly to you. You are the mother now. And, over time, this new earthly relationship will bring forth greater depths to the eternal relationship you have with each other, which is the one that matters most.

«« Q »»
I worry about dying and going to heaven because I have been married twice. I loved both of them. What happens when I get to heaven and have two husbands there?

The legal relationships of couples belong to this physical, earthly realm. When we are in heaven, we can maintain these loving relationships if we choose. The legal commitments do not carry over from earth to heaven. You are with people in heaven because you want to be: because you love them and enjoy spending time together.

Freedom is valued on earth and in heaven. In heaven, you are free to spend time with your two husbands as you and they choose. You are also free to form other relationships.

If you love each other and want to be together, you can certainly maintain the relationships. But the relationships in heaven are different. On earth, couples traditionally used to marry because they were going to start a family. They were providing a commitment to each other, and a home for the raising of children. There was stability in marriage: social, legal and financial. You don't need this kind of stability in heaven, because these needs belong to the earthly realm.

You have tremendous stability and security in heaven. You feel so secure that you don't even think about it! You have an expectation of well-being for yourself and your loved ones.

There are none of the negative earthly emotions for you to worry about. Your husbands would not feel jealous of one another. There is no jealousy in heaven. They would each spend time with you, if you want them to. In heaven, they have in common the fact that they love you. And in heaven, that is quite meaningful. It would mean nothing negative to them that they both loved you. They might even be friends because they have someone in common that they care about. Your first husband would be glad that you found someone else to enjoy life with. Your second husband would be happy that you had companionship until he arrived in your life. They would not see it as a problem that you had been married twice. They understand that there are no earthly limitations in heaven. There is no shortage of love.

It is not an issue in heaven at all that you have been married twice. This is your eternal home you are returning to. You probably don't want to hear this, but there may be other men there that you have loved in other lives, prior to this earthly lifetime. There are also beings there that you have connected with strictly in the non-physical realm. Love is amazing. Real, unconditional love as it is experienced in heaven is abundant. You can love many people at the same time.

On earth, when we are parents, we may have many children and love them all. We can't imagine that we would only love one child at a time, or that we would have to end a relationship with one child to create an opening to love another child. We know that our heart is capable of great love.

Legal relationships that bind two people together belong to the earthly realm, not to heaven. There is no expectation there that you can love only one man. Relationships in heaven are about love. They are not about raising children. They are not about social, legal or financial obligations. They are not about committing to each other to stay together through the hard times as well as the good: in heaven there are only good times! In heaven, relationships are simply about love.

You say you loved both of these men. And it seems they loved you, too. In heaven, you will have a great time. You will enjoy seeing each other. You will appreciate the pleasure of each other's company. You will celebrate your love, and continue to take that love in each relationship to new heights. Your bond with each of these men will continue to grow and prosper. There is absolutely nothing for you to be concerned about.

«« Q »»
Do animals go to heaven?

Heaven simply wouldn't be heaven without the animals so many of us love so much.

There is no doubt that dogs and cats, and *all* of our beloved animals, go to heaven. We are reunited with them when *we* go there. They will have a good time there without us, and they will continue to have a wonderful time when we join them.

The bonds of love are timeless and eternal. We often do not spend just one lifetime with our animals. Often, we may incarnate numerous times, and find each other again and again, wherever we are located on this planet. If you ever saw an animal that you felt an instant bond with, it is possible that you are not just finding that animal for the first time, but you are reuniting with each other.

Death is not an end. It is simply a transition. When an animal you love dies, the spirit of that animal – that animal's soul, if you will – is simply leaving that particular physical body, that particular physical lifetime. The animal's soul, like your soul, is eternal and will continue to live. Your separation from each other is merely temporary.

So you never really say goodbye. All you say is, "Until we meet again." Because if you love each other, there is no doubt that you will meet again.

After the spirit of your beloved animal departs the physical body, it is also possible you will find that the animal's spirit continues to be present with you sometimes, continues to be close. In your grief, you may not be able to connect with your animal because the spirit of the animal is now in a state of bliss. But if you allow yourself, you may find times that you feel your animal close. You may see your animal out of the corner of your eye. You may feel your animal with you, especially when you are just waking up in the morning or drifting off to sleep at night. Those are times when we tend to be more connected to the non-physical realm, and less connected to the beliefs that keep us separate from God and our loved ones.

My mother's cats used to sleep with her on her bed every night. And after they made their transitions to the non-physical world, she would often feel them there with her when she would wake up in the middle of the night or early morning. Some people might have said these were simply her memories "playing tricks" on her. But she knew better. She could "feel" the cats there, "sense" them there, and there was no denying her experience.

That we are separated from our loved ones in death is a myth. It is our belief that we cannot be together that keeps us apart, and it is a false belief. Remember the good times you shared with your loved ones, remember the love you felt, remember the joy, and you may find them right here with you.

«« Q »»

I love animals. All animals. I always have. I think it's easier to relate to them than people. It has always bothered me to see the bodies of dead animals on the roads when I am driving. It feels like each of those deaths is a needless tragedy. It upsets me and can get my whole day off to a bad start. Do you have any suggestions about how I can cope with this better?

The situation you are describing is upsetting to many people. It seems unlikely that this condition is going entirely away, so it is important to reframe the way you are thinking about it.

Many people are starting to consider animals when building roadways, and are creating passages for the animals to safely cross the roads. More of this will occur in the future. More people are recognizing that we share this planet and are interconnected in many ways. Even if they don't care about the animals, they realize there are drivers who will try to avoid hitting animals on the roads. Animals will always seek food and shelter, and try to find it in new areas when they can't locate it near them. Better to provide safe passages for the animals to cross, to keep them off the road surfaces when possible.

Now, as you point out, these are dead bodies along the roads. They are no longer the animals themselves. They are the shells the animals were living in while they were having earthly experiences. The spirits of these animals have left these bodies. The bodies used to be inhabited by these animals but they are no more. These animals' spirits have re-emerged to heaven, to a better place.

What bothers many people is the violent way these earthly experiences ended. It's important to realize that many of these are wild animals. In the wild, their physical lives are often ended by predators who see the animals as food. This is a part of the cycle of physical life. Animals rarely lie down and say, "Come eat me." They will fight for

99

their continued physical existence. They will fight to survive. Deaths in the wild are rarely peaceful. Many animals' physical experiences end due to the weather and other, what would be considered natural, conditions. Cars and other vehicles have simply become the new predators. In many ways, the abrupt death animals can experience from a vehicle may be faster than what they might experience in the wild. That may not be a comforting thought, but it is reality.

Now, you often see the bodies of companion animals on the roads, too. What is important with all of these animal bodies is to realize these are merely the shells that are left behind. Their spirits are in a much better place now. And rather than give your attention to the way these animals met the end of their physical experiences, you can choose to consider where those animals are in this present moment.

It is logical that anyone would prefer a peaceful death over a violent one. But it is also true that many people, even if they do not have violent deaths, do not have peaceful experiences of dying. Direct your focus to the joyful experience the animal is having now. See the age of the body as an indicator of accomplishment, of how long that animal was able to avoid predators and other threats. These animals' spirits in heaven are not distressed about the way their earthly experiences came to an end. You don't need to be, either.

There are also occasions where animals will choose death in a way that a human might choose suicide. They don't feel well, their bodies aren't working anymore, and they are ready to re-emerge back into the non-physical realm. So try not to grieve for the experience the animals had. Try to rejoice for the fact these animals had earthly lives. They are now in a joyful place, experiencing the benefits that were created through the expansion of desire that came from those physical lives. Consider that these animals will make new starts when ready, and come in again with brand new, fully functioning bodies.

Think about the beings who love each of these animals and with whom they were reunited upon returning to heaven, or will be someday. This is no different than a body in a coffin at a funeral, and many people make an intentional choice to see that. This is one physical experience concluded, but a new chapter in the life of this animal has begun. Be joyful for this animal. Send love if you choose. Wish the spirit of the animal well. But don't use the way its physical experience ended as a source of grief that will separate you from who you really are. Your feelings are coming about because of a misunderstanding of death. Join this animal in the playful joy it is now experiencing in the non-physical realm. Be happy. A wonderful new chapter in the eternal life of that animal has begun.

«« Q »»
I have always thought I wouldn't like heaven
because I like to be busy.

Well, you are dealing with a common preconception of heaven, and a misconception. Sure, the idea of lying around amidst the clouds sounds like heaven to some people – and hell to others. But that is not what heaven is.

You can be busy all the time in heaven, or not busy at all. You have the freedom to be as busy, or not, as you want to be. The choice is entirely yours.

Being busy in heaven is about focus. It is up to you to choose what you want to focus on.

There are not the earthly responsibilities of caring for a physical body in heaven, not your own body's well-being or the bodies of others. In heaven, you are a being of energy. You do not have a physical body that needs tending the way it does here.

But you still can enjoy the earthly activities you enjoy here, and many more. There are many things you love to do here that you can continue to do in heaven. And there are many more things to do in heaven than there are here. Some of them are just different. Some of them are the same as here, but you do them in different ways.

If you like to go skiing or snowboarding or skateboarding, for example, the way you undertake the activity is to focus on it and imagine yourself doing it, and then you ARE doing it.

The way you travel is to imagine the place you want to be, and then you are there. You don't have to worry about transportation. You don't need money to buy a ticket. You just envision yourself there and you are there, in the midst of the experience.

Can you see that there are many opportunities available to you in heaven?

You focus upon the experience you want to have, and you have it. Focus is the key.

Indeed, focus is a lot more important here on earth than we usually recognize. But it is crucial in heaven, and you will be able to do it easily there. So if you are someone who experiences what is considered an attention "disorder" on earth, please realize that you will not have that issue in heaven. That condition is greatly misunderstood here on earth, and if you still experience it on earth before you die, you will not experience it in heaven.

If you like being busy here on earth, you can continue to be busy in heaven. And if you are tired of being really busy here on earth and you want to rest in heaven, you can do that, too. If you want to rest and then get busy again with activities you really like, you can do that. The important thing to realize is that your level of activity in heaven is a CHOICE. There is no right or wrong. There is no one standing over you telling you to do something. You have the freedom to be as busy – or unbusy – as you choose. Heaven is happy...whatever that is for you.

«« Q »»

I believe that when we die, our individual consciousness re-emerges with the larger consciousness of All That Is. But when we do that, we lose our individuality. I think of it as pouring a cup of water back into the ocean. That cup of water gets mixed in with the water of the ocean. So I do believe that I don't die, I don't end; I just am not myself anymore. Do I lose my personality, my uniqueness, when I die? Will I still exist as me?

You are correct that there is a larger consciousness. In the non-physical world, we exist as energetic bodies, and not in physical bodies as we do here on earth. Except even on earth, we are connected to that larger consciousness. Here, we have forgotten that connection exists. Sometimes we are reminded of it. But mostly, we live as individual selves who feel separate from one another.

Because we perceive the world through our physical bodies here on earth, we see where our bodies end and other bodies begin. Most of us do not see energetic bodies. We don't see the field of energy that exists in and around our physical bodies. This also perpetuates the idea of separateness.

At the non-physical level, you are aware of the connection. But you are still you. You don't have the resistant thoughts that keep you feeling isolated. Here, we have the perception that we are separate. But it is a false perception. We perpetuate it because it is what we believe. But that connection to the larger consciousness exists here as in the non-physical world. We just don't acknowledge it and access it. In the non-physical world, we do.

Scientists who study quantum physics acknowledge, more and more, that the space which seems to be empty between us is actually alive and filled. Space is a living thing. It is not empty.

You are part of the larger consciousness here on earth. And you will be part of that same consciousness in heaven. The difference is that most people here are not aware they are part of something much bigger than themselves. In the non-physical realm, we know.

You still exist as you at the non-physical level. You are different, because you are not spending most of your time thinking resistant thoughts. You are experiencing love, joy, understanding, and total acceptance. You are enjoying the thrill of the ride.

How does my loved one feel about me disposing
of items that used to hold special meaning?

When you are in the physical realm, physical items can hold tremendous meaning. We can attach great sentimentality to material possessions. It is not the item so much that holds special value: it is the meaning attached to it. This meaning may be a positive memory; it may hold special significance because it indicates an achievement that was a source of great pride. It may be that someone we loved gave us something, and that item brought back recollections of that person, time and place.

The joy of life is in the creation of it. Especially as people grow older, they often look back on the positive aspects of what they created. Good memories of the past can become as meaningful as the present. But the meaning attached to all of these items is coming from the expression of the person in the physical realm.

Once we pass into the non-physical realm, we let those attachments go. The place that we move to, heaven, holds such great joy. And there is so much to do there. We easily release those physical associations with our earthly lives. We understand the eternalness of life and the eternal nature of our own being. It would be impractical to hold onto everything that was special, to bring it from one life to the next. It is not an issue to people in the non-physical realm that you dispose of the items that once held meaning to them. Do these items hold meaning to you? Will they enhance the quality of your own life now? Selling or giving away things that were meaningful to your loved one here on earth does not cause your loved one distress in heaven. After all: it is heaven! If you keep things on earth out of a feeling of guilt or obligation, it does not enhance your life. It doesn't make your loved one feel any more special or valued.

The possession of things is part of what most of us create in our earthly lives. But these things belong to this earthly place. It is okay to let go of items that were meaningful to your loved one if you choose. And it is okay to hold onto them if they have enough meaning for you that they enhance your present life. Your loved one is in a place of such joy and understanding. You will not offend or dishonor. They understand you have your own life to live. They also understand that they will be coming back, and that they get to create a physical experience all over again. What is meaningful to them in their last physical life may not be desired in their next physical life. The cycle of life is, indeed, eternal.

Is it silly that I talk to my loved one who died?
Can I communicate with someone who is dead?

You can't communicate with someone who is "ended." But since there isn't dead and we never end, that means the spirit of your loved one is still alive. And if you want to communicate, then you can.

The spirit of someone in the non-physical world is an expansive, joyful version of who they really are. Earthly life takes a toll on most people: it wears them down. The soul of someone in non-physical is like taking the very best of a person and then seeing that best develop fully. It is a wonderful, almost miraculous thing. All of the fears and resistance that a person developed in the course of his or her life leaves instantly at the moment of death.

So, if someone dies and I want to communicate with that person, I need to be in a joyful place to be able to connect. If I am miserable and grieving because I miss the person's physical presence, I cannot communicate. We are on two very different frequencies. I have to be happy to communicate, because my loved one is in a place of great joy. I also have to allow myself to experience my loved one as he or she is now, and not reduce that person to a past memory.

Souls are timeless and ageless. If you knew someone who died while living in a child's body, you are looking to communicate with a fully expansive soul. Children are not less mature souls than adults. A soul that has extended into a baby's body may not be experienced in the ways of earthly life at that moment, but is fully experienced in all aspects of non-physical life. Children, even infants, go to the other side as the fully expanded souls they really are.

Children often come forth to teach us. It is a misconception that we, as adults, are here to teach them. Children can be powerful spiritual teachers. Children may die for many different reasons. Sometimes, they only want a short, intense physical experience. Often, the seemingly short time of their physical experience sets us off on a deeper search about the meaning of life and death. Their death inspired us to achieve a greater spiritual understanding of the timeless nature of life and love. Since relationships are eternal when we want them to be, we will be with our loved ones again.

Communicating with someone in the non-physical realm can be very easy. It is simply a matter of conversing with them. You don't need special equipment or training. But, to go back to what I mentioned earlier about being happy: your energy must be on a frequency close enough to your loved one's that you can communicate.

If you are feeling really happy, you have a chance. If you are sad or grieving, your vibrational frequencies are too far apart to communicate.

Our loved ones usually want to communicate with us after they have crossed back into non-physical. We are the ones making it difficult, not them.

So, if you want to communicate, the first thing you need to do is get happy. At the very least, be in a state where you feel peaceful and content.

Then think of your loved one. Think positive thoughts of your loved one.

Allow yourself to "hear" your loved one communicate with you.

Thoughts are energy: electrical impulses. Your loved ones can communicate with you through thought.

You will hear their words internally. Some people might say they "hear" the words in their head. Others might say they "hear" the words in their heart or their solar plexus.

You won't hear them talking aloud to you outside your body. There won't be disembodied voices coming through to you in the room. You will receive their thoughts in your mind and translate them into words.

You have to trust yourself to do this. At first, you may get simple answers or statements. As you get used to the frequency, and trust that what you are receiving is accurate, you will strengthen the connection with your loved one. As you do, you will be able to have communication with your loved one much as you used to converse here on earth.

Your loved one may seem smarter to you than you remember. Your loved one's vocabulary may be bigger. You are communicating with your loved one as your loved one is now, having a stronger connection with his or her God-self.

If you are tuning into your loved one and hear something negative, perhaps a negative comment or emotion, then you are tuning into something else, perhaps your memory of that person and his or her ghost energy. You are not tuning into that person now in heaven. Your loved one in heaven will be positively focused. Don't limit your loved one to the way you remember him or her. Your loved one has become more expansive in death. You need to allow that.

Your loved one will be happily active in heaven. So if your loved one doesn't answer you right away, it may be because he or she is involved in something else at the moment.

The best advice is: just start talking to your loved one. And then relax and listen: allow yourself to receive your loved one's response. Don't doubt yourself, or feel like you have to try hard. Don't become frustrated if it doesn't happen right away. Just trust that it will happen with time.

You don't need to expend a lot of effort at this. Developing a pattern of communication comes with practice. Learning to do this is a process for most people that happens over time. Be patient with yourself. If you get angry or frustrated with yourself because it isn't happening as quickly as you like, then you are moving out of happiness and away from the vibration of your loved one in heaven.

It is also important to know that your loved one may communicate with you through other means, just to let you know that he or she is nearby. Sometimes, loved ones will work in concert with animals or insects or children to give us signs. For instance, you might see a butterfly when you are thinking about a departed sister. Your wife's favorite bird might be inspired to fly into your view when you are thinking about her. The phone might ring yet no one is there. A light in the room might flash on and off. A child might be inspired to bring you a photo or trinket, or draw a picture with special meaning.

Our loved ones may speak to us through feelings. We might feel someone close, feel a hug from the inside, feel like they are there with us. We might not be able to describe the feeling of having them close, in words, but we know it when we feel it.

Loved ones can also contact us through dreams. We may talk in the dreams, enjoy a feeling of closeness, or resolve old issues. We might simply recognize through the dream that our loved one is still alive.

Music is also a common way of communicating. You might find yourself hearing a tune in your head that you associate with your loved one. Perhaps your loved one sings you a favorite tune in the non-physical realm and you find yourself singing or humming it to yourself, seemingly out-of-the-blue. Perhaps you are thinking of your loved one, and are inspired to tune the radio to a particular station where you find a special song. They are letting you know that they are here with you.

Be open to these messages. Once you accept their desire to communicate with you, you will find these messages come much more often that you ever anticipated.

I have studied and studied the pictures of my husband and tried to communicate with him since he died. I am not having any luck at all. Do you have any suggestions?

Well, first: ease up. You are trying too hard! You are making work out of something that is really very easy to do.

Second, stop focusing on the fact that you can't do it. Because you can. There is no doubt at all that you can.

Third, breathe and relax. Be easy with it.

By studying so intently the picture of your husband, you are focusing on who he was in the past – not on who he is, where he is, how he is *now*. You have to let him be who he is now. By remembering who he was in his previous life with you, you are restricting your access.

You are talking about communicating with his soul as he is now, in the present. He is a more expanded being than you remember. Even if he was an angel on earth, he was subject to earthly stressors that are no longer a part of his experience. He is more allowing now of a connection to God. He is wiser and more loving than you remember.

Let me offer a metaphor. Imagine two rooms that are connected by a door. The room you are in is dark. The other room, where your husband is now, is brightly lit. You want to let the light into your room. But you only open the door to your husband's room a sliver, just a little bit. What you need to do is allow the door to swing open fully, and truly know him as he is now. As long as you are expecting him to be as he was, you are keeping his light from coming through as brilliantly as he is now. You can't "see" him if you only open the door a little bit. Let the door open wide.

Ask your husband to communicate with you. He undoubtedly already knows you have been trying. And then: let it go. Focus on other things. Some people experience communication, at least at first, through non-verbal means. Perhaps you are out on a walk and see a dragonfly that reminds you of him. Yes, he sent it. You might be thinking of him· and the light flickers in the room. Perhaps you smell the fragrance of his after-shave lotion. You might be doing housework and find yourself singing a song that reminds you of him, because he is singing that song in your ear. Let yourself feel the fullness of who he is now. That is a great start.

When you stop trying so hard to hear him, and instead just allow the presence of him to get fuller, you will find yourself able to have conversations with him. Trust yourself when this happens. You will know.

And remember: he is communicating with you, too. You have to allow *who he is now* to be the one who answers.

«« Q »»
How should I talk to my children about death?

When children are ready to learn about death, they will usually ask you about it.

They will voice their curiosity. More importantly, how you talk about death and act towards death will serve as a model for them, as you are already modeling for them on many subjects.

When children ask you questions about death, it is important to answer just what they ask, on the level they ask it. If a beloved pet dies, a child might ask, "Will I see my pet again?" You can answer, "Yes, you will see your pet in heaven. And the spirit of your pet might visit you here on earth too.

If a six-year old asks about death, you might explain that the spirit lives forever, but sometimes the spirit lives in a body and sometimes it lives in heaven. When someone dies, the spirit leaves the body and goes to heaven. Someday the spirit will come back to earth in another body. You might take a glove and put it on your hand, explaining that the hand is like the soul and it goes into the body, which is like a glove here on earth. When we say that someone dies, it means the soul leaves the body, but it is still alive in heaven.

If a twelve-year-old asks, you could add that when someone dies, it is a lot like God is recycling the body. We leave a physical body that is energy. The body is transformed to another form of energy. That energy is used to create other things. Bodies that are buried in the earth, or their ashes, eventually become soil. What were once our bodies become nourishment for the earth, where we live, where plants grow to replenish the air we breathe and nourish our bodies – and the cycle continues.

Some young people might also understand that while a part of us comes to earth, our God-self always remains in

114

heaven. It is accessible to us here on earth at all times, but it remains in heaven. That is the loving and wise "little voice" we hear inside sometimes – or a lot. It is the source of our intuition and "gut feelings." It is the joy and love we feel when we are engaged in thoughts or actions that are aligned with God.

It is important to understand that children, when born, come in knowing what death really is. Through their contact with us, we un-teach them. They un-learn what they came in knowing. Small children often remember details of their previous lives. They might remember occupations, places they lived, or even relationships from previous lives: "Mommy, you were my baby once." Young children often see the energy of spirits who visit us and know how to interpret it: "Look, there's Grandma!" or "Fluffy came to see me last night."

We can learn a lot from our children if we realize how much they know, and how much they have to teach us. They are not "blank slates" when they are born. They have forgotten much of their past physical lives so they can embrace this one fully. But they know more about the non-physical experience than most of us remember, in part because they have just come from there. Why do we find babies so heavenly? That is where they are coming from.

I have heard that people's spirits often attend
their own funeral. Is this true?

Imagine that people you really care about are all going to gather together. Imagine they are going to talk about you in loving and complimentary ways. Wouldn't you want to be there? Where else on earth could you see so many people you love all at once?

Yes, most people do attend their own memorial or celebration of life service.

I have often thought it is amusing when people say they are not going to a funeral because the deceased person is not going to be there. That's a big misconception!

Now, will the "dead person" think less of you because you don't go? Of course not. Will it hurt their feelings if you don't attend? Not at all. In fact, many of them would quite prefer you were doing something else – having fun, or celebrating them in a joyful way – instead of engaging in an activity that would bring you grief.

At my husband's funeral, when the family was lead up to the front row of the church to be seated, right by my husband's body in the coffin, I thought it was too overwhelming. I understood fully, for the first time, why my mother wanted to leave her brother's funeral in the middle of the service. She said it was simply too hard.

As I sat there in the moments before the service for my husband began, I felt a spiritual calm descend upon me. It is difficult to describe in words. It was a feeling of intense peace. The grief left, and a deep loving peace overtook me. I felt like I had been blessed with a powerful, benevolent spiritual presence. A gift.

Then I heard my husband's voice. My husband used to like to repeat words back to people exactly as they had spoken them. He repeated back to me the words I had used in a conversation with him months before he died. We had been sitting in the living room one day, discussing a friend of his who had passed away. I said to him, "You know, most people attend their own funerals."

And, as I sat in that church on the day of his funeral, he said, "You told me that most people attend their own funerals. Well, I'm here."

I understand now that if I had not been in a place of such calm, he could not have communicated with me. I had been powerfully asking for help to deal with his funeral. In that moment, I was given a gift of peace that allowed me to hear him.

That was the first time after his death that I felt him with me. There have been many times since.

Yes, people attend their own funerals. My husband attended his. I am sure of it.

Section III: Dementia

Chapter 7
Dementia: Toward a New Understanding

Dementia is a gradual softening of focus on the physical life that one has created on earth. It is a way to gently release the attachment to one's earthly life, in preparation for re-emergence to the non-physical world.

It is intended, rather than being a dis-ease, to help bring ease. It occurs because of dis-ease.

Dementia is not a punishment or an indicator that anyone has done something wrong. There should be no shame in having dementia. That's not what it is about.

What I am offering here is a spiritual perspective on dementia: why it exists spiritually, and how we can better work with people who have it. There are many physicians and researchers who offer medical and scientific explanations. And for medical understanding and assistance, you should certainly turn to them.

But sometimes, people are asking a larger *why*: why is there dementia? Why does my loved one have it? Why do I have it? That is what I am trying to address here: to offer an opinion from a spiritual perspective.

People have dementia for many reasons. There is no one-size-fits-all answer. A common reason is an internal conflict about what happens at the time of death. There can be strong fear, even terror, about what is perceived as the unknown. And a feeling that one must cling to earthly life as long as possible, postponing what is so feared. Others simply don't want to let go. Sometimes, they have felt a need to be in control for a long time. It can be hard to release one's self to the strengthening call of one's God-self, back to the non-physical realm. When you have been struggling to be in control for decades, it can be challenging to release that control and *allow*.

Sometimes, the process of dementia begins by gradually releasing details that are unnecessary in the non-physical world, but that we find important here. For instance, the memory or recognition of dates, months, years, names and places might lapse. These belong to earthly life.

In heaven, we recognize each other energetically. Everyone's energy is unique. We do not need a name in order to locate or recognize someone. In the same way, someone with dementia may "know" who a person is without attaching a name or relationship to that person. A person with dementia may see each person strictly from the present moment. They may recognize the essence of that being, and perhaps why that person is there at that moment. For instance, if the person is there to feed a meal, the individual with dementia may recognize and attach that activity to that person – or not, depending on where someone is in the process.

Dementia is an extended process. It is not something with a fixed timeline attached. It is not something that happens suddenly, with its full impact being felt immediately. It is gradual.

Someone may become partially disengaged from earthly life, or more fully disengaged, before re-emerging back into heaven.

How long it takes is very individual. When people are ready to die – truly ready – they die: they re-emerge into heaven. Until then, it is likely that the dementia will seem to strengthen over an extended period of time. Specifically, it means someone will gradually become more disengaged from earthly life.

There are the initial signs of disengagement. Most people are usually aware that they are starting to become more forgetful. Contrary to how society reacts, this is actually not a bad thing. It is a change. But it is not bad, in and of itself. It just no longer meets social expectations that one's mind is "sharp" and that we remember certain things.

Our society has very strong expectations around a "good" memory. I have met many healthy young individuals who feel they possess a personal weakness because there is something specific they do not tend to remember well. Many people forget names, or have difficulty matching names with faces and where their relationship with a certain acquaintance has come from. Even though they remember people close to them who are currently active in their lives, their memory may not always be strong about everything.

Since we start teaching children very early the importance of memorization, we have to recognize that memory is a concept on which our society places great value. We expect children's memory will become better as they grow older.

What we see with aging adults is often the reverse process of what children experience. As children form attachments to an earthly life, their memory grows. They come from heaven without any need for some of the information we on earth consider so vital.

As adults prepare to return to heaven, they can release these attachments. In fact, it is easier for many of them, as they prepare to return, to let go of these attachments. Most of this memory will not serve them once they get into heaven, and preserving these attachments can make the transition from the physical world more difficult.

«« Q »»
So if my loved one has forgotten who I am on earth,
will she remember me in heaven?

Of course! Forgetting your name, or even your present relationship, is part of this *earthly* process of letting go. But your relationship with your loved one is eternal. The God-self of your loved one knows you, and will always know you. So does the spirit-self of your loved one. You will be together again. Earthly memory has absolutely nothing to do with our eternal relationships. Let me repeat this: earthly memory has nothing to do with eternal relationships.

Part of the reason that your loved one's seeming forgetfulness is painful to you is because the God-self part of you knows that what you are thinking is incorrect. Your loved one has not forgotten you. Your loved one is simply letting go of all earthly attachments to ease into a re-emergence to the non-physical world. Your loved one, on a spirit level, still knows you. Your loved one, on a spirit level, knows you will be together again. There is no question that any separation will be temporary. When you are looking at time from a place of eternity, what we see from earth as months or years or even decades are like a tiny blink. They mean very little in the grand picture.

Children are born with very little memory of their previous lives on earth. They have some knowing of the past, and that knowledge is available to them. But they are here to live NOW. They are here to focus on creating an earthly life NOW. The present is what is important to them, not the past.

Likewise, what we see with people who have dementia is that the past becomes unimportant. What matters is NOW. They relate to the present more and more as the process evolves, without the distraction of the past. What happened yesterday becomes irrelevant, as does what happened five, ten, fifty years ago. What happened an hour ago eventually becomes irrelevant. They are living, fully, in the present moment. If we pay attention to them, they can teach us how better to do this ourselves.

I know so many people who are always dragging the past into their present. They take the unhappy moments of their past and relive them over and over. They keep recreating the past, reliving the past in the present.

Now, even people who fully engage with life from the present moment may start to soften their focus on their present life. They are still finding some value in living, in continuing to perceive life from the perspective of a physical body. But even those who connect only with the present may eventually start to relax that focus and withdraw from present experience. There is still an attachment to the physical body, but that attachment softens.

To illustrate this point more clearly, think about times in your life that you were happiest, most engaged, felt most fully alive. We usually feel an increased vitality during these times. We are drawing more life-force energy, and we feel more energy flowing though us. These are the moments of passion, of intense living, that most of us love to have and love to remember. It is one of the reasons, for instance, that wartime experiences are so vivid. I have heard many people, considered physically elderly, talk about their military experiences as young adults in war with great vivacity. They felt fully alive in some of those moments. They may not have been "good" moments as we define them, but they felt larger than other moments in their lives.

It is this same strengthening of energy that we often feel when we are falling in love with someone. It is one of the reasons that falling in love can feel so great, when the relationship itself may seem later to require much more effort. Falling in love can be easy, and can feel very, very good. These are different moments with differing kinds of intensity, but an intensity of living, nonetheless.

«« *Q* »»
But I want my loved one to be the way I remember her.
I miss my loved one, even though my loved one is still, technically, alive.

Your loved one has changed. It is doubtful that she will return to the way you remember her being. There may be moments she is closer to what you remember. But as the process continues, those moments are likely to get fewer and farther apart.

It is important not to view dementia as a failing on her part, or even as an illness. It is a way of coping and preparing. It is a way of preparing to make the return to the non-physical realm. It does not mean you are not still loved, or loved less. Your loved one is actually moving forward in her journey, not backward.

We think of people reaching a certain level of vitality in life. They are bright, full of life, and perhaps have accomplished many things they intended. We often look at life as a straight line with an arrow at the end – and the person is supposed to keep moving in that direction. Anything different we consider a failing.

For people who develop dementia, life is much more circular. After reaching that peak, they are returning to a more child-like state of innocence, of living in the present moment. If you could envision the starting point of drawing a circle as the entry into this earthly life through birth, the circle expands as they live life and closes with a return to that starting point. There has been great complexity in life: great expansion. Now there is a return to simplicity. The person's life circle is nearing completion. For people with dementia, the journey of life is more circular than linear.

When we have enjoyed certain aspects of someone, it is natural to want them to continue to be there. But people change. We have all known individuals that we enjoyed doing a certain activity with, but then they stopped participating in that activity for some reason. We missed them. We missed engaging in that activity with them. But our lives did not end, nor did theirs. You have to remember that your loved one is in a spiral of eternal life. The earthly life your loved one has been living is coming to completion, but the eternal life you share is not. You will share more lifetimes together. You will share those activities in other physical bodies. You may even share those activities together in the non-physical world. This is not a permanent end. This is simply a transition.

It is natural to grieve, to miss aspects of your loved one or things you did together. But it is important to let that go and be with your loved one in the present. That is what your loved one is doing. Live for the present, in the present, with your loved one. Don't look backward except as those memories might provide you with comfort, and as a reminder of what you will share again in the future, in future lives.

«« Q »»

But I want my loved one to be the same as before. I get angry with him that he isn't, and I keep trying to make him be different, like he used to be.

People with dementia are happiest when the people around them love them unconditionally. In fact, that is one of the important lessons to be learned. If you do love this person, then now is an opportunity for you to practice unconditional love.

Unconditional love means loving without strings. You don't place conditions on your love. You don't say, "I only love you when you are this way, or act that way." Unconditional love, the kind of love that God feels for us, is total loving acceptance of who we are. You don't try to change someone. You accept who the person is now and keep loving. You may not love the conditions, but you look through the conditions to love the person.

You have to let go of who your loved one was in the past. Remembering does not serve either of you. You will keep being angry, and will keep expressing anger, not love. You

127

can't feel anger and love at the same time. You can't be unhappy with who he is now and still love him.

If you really love this person, try to be in the present with him. Try to experience the world the way he does now. You have to let go of the past, as he is.

You also have to stop controlling him. Stop trying to remake him into someone he no longer is. That is who you want him to be, but that is not who he is anymore.

When people with dementia express anger, it is often *toward* someone who is trying to control them–or *when* someone is trying to control them. Like a child, they usually know what they want. They know what they want and they want it now, in the present moment. The easiest thing for both of you is to let your loved one have what he wants when he wants it.

Now, there are times you might intervene, when someone's personal safety is at risk, for example. I know you are going to stop someone from wandering into a road busy with traffic. But if you have someone who is at a physical age of ninety and wants to watch cartoons on television instead of the sports he always enjoyed so much, let him watch cartoons. Don't try to control him. Don't fight him to become the way you remember. In the present moment, he wants to watch cartoons. He finds enjoyment in them now, even if he hasn't before.

If he wants to carry a comforting, non-harmful item with him when he goes to the store with you, let him have it. If he wants to wear a shirt and pants that don't match, let him. You can tell people that he picked out his clothes that day if it embarrasses you. It is not your job to control him. It is your job to love him.

Let him be happy. Love him and let him be happy. That is your work now. Let him be the way he is. Let him be who he is now. Allow yourself to find reasons to love him now, the way he is.

Many people late in the cycle of dementia are very sweet, loving, happy people. It can be like looking at the spirit of a very young child in a grown body.

I have watched people with dementia in nursing homes. Some of them wander, and it is interesting to watch where they wander: into rooms where they feel good. They go into rooms where people are laughing, not where people are angry. They go into rooms that are quiet, not noisy. They go into rooms with comfortable furniture, not hard furniture. They prefer rooms that are pretty to rooms that are ugly. They know what feels good to them, and they seek that out.

I have also seen spouses and adult children who were trying to "take care of" their loved ones by doing what they thought was the right thing to do, even if it was against their loved one's wishes. Their loved one would become angry, even enraged, and would fight them. They did not want anyone trying to control them.

Very young children are quite sensitive to people – adults and other children – who try to control them. As they grow older, they get used to adults trying to control them and being displeased with them or punishing them if they resist that control. It often seems easier to the children to learn to accommodate others and adjust behavior. People with dementia can be like those very young children who are simply seeking freedom.

Freedom is a fundamental human desire. We all want as much freedom as we can enjoy. We want freedom to express and satisfy our desires through our minds, our lives, our bodies. Children want that. Adults want that. People with dementia want that.

Do what you can to ensure that the people in your life with dementia have as much freedom as possible over the things that matter to them. They may not be the same things that once mattered. But see how much control you can relinquish, and therefore return, to your loved one. You will both be much happier in the time you have left together in this particular cycle of earthly life.

«« Q »»

The hardest part for me of visiting my father at his nursing home is leaving at the end of the visit. I just want to wrap him up in my arms and bring him home. And I know I can't. I can't safely care for him.

It is natural for you to feel this way, even though it feels painful to you. It speaks of your love for your father, and your desire to take care of him.

There are several important things to remember to help you cope when you leave. First of all, even though it is hard to leave, I imagine it is harder on you than it is on your father. His dementia is protecting him, in a sense, from feeling what you feel. And even if he does feel it momentarily, he is likely to forget and get distracted by something else much faster than you are.

Second, I would not think your father would want to be a burden to you. Even though he may not be as happy in a nursing home as he would have been in his own home, you know that is no longer a possibility for him. You have put him in the best possible facility you could find and afford. You believe the staff cares for and about him, or I imagine you would keep searching for another facility. I have seen the families of other residents come to care greatly about the people they see regularly. They also watch out for them and help them. So he may not be as alone as you think he is, or as you feel he is.

Third, even though he may be in emotional distress at times, his distress is not as severe as you may be projecting onto him. I am not trying to minimize it or take it away. Distress is distress. But you have all your mental capabilities, and your father no longer does.

130

Perhaps what you are recognizing and feeling, most importantly, is his lack of connection to God, to Source. People with dementia are typically not feeling a strong connection to the non-physical world, and to all the love that is there for them. Whether we have dementia or not, we feel most disconnected ourselves when we feel disconnected from God. You are recognizing his disconnection when you see his loneliness.

No matter how religious he was in his earlier life, he is not feeling a spiritual connection now or he would not feel so alone and so helpless. I am guessing that you are also not feeling that connection, or you would not be feeling that helplessness when you leave him. If you can reconnect to God yourself, you will find it easier to relate to your father from a point of connection. You will find it easier to leave because you know he is not alone. There is great love present for your father in the non-physical world. There are also many loved ones who are already in the non-physical world that are watching out for him and regularly visiting him. He is never truly alone.

You see him alone, vulnerable and powerless. That is also how he probably came to feel himself in his later years.

He has an always-present connection to the non-physical, spiritual world. He may not have let himself feel this connection and this love for a very long time. But it is still there, and it is still available to him.

When you leave, you are looking through your earthly eyes at a physical situation. You are not seeing the larger part of him that is reaching out to him from the non-physical. You are not seeing the love and the loved ones who surround him. He is not alone. He may feel alone because he is not connecting to them. But when you see him as lonely, you are also not recognizing that connection.

The larger part of your father has remained in the non-physical world and the part of him that is projected here will eventually re-emerge with that larger part. His sense of disconnection from that larger part of himself has become your reason for disconnection. There is love that surrounds him and is available to him at all times.

Sometimes, our loved ones use us as a distraction from their loneliness for that spiritual connection. Sometimes they find that connection through us, because they can see how much we love and care for them. When we leave their presence, we see them lose it. Then we can end up feeling responsible, if we allow ourselves, for them not being happier.

If your father felt that connection, he would probably not be where he is now. If he felt that love and comfort that is available to him from non-physical, he would not be feeling alone and powerless. Fear often creates feelings of loneliness, vulnerability and helplessness.

He may feel your love for him. But he is also seeking to feel the love of God. Telling him about it won't help now: but he is seeking, on some level, to feel it. You can love him, but you can't replace what he is disconnected from. Nor is it your job to do. You cannot help connect him, except perhaps temporarily. He is seeking a stronger, more permanent connection. In your heart, you want that for him too, which is why it is hard to leave him without seeing him achieve it.

Remind yourself when you leave that you are not leaving him alone. There are many people there from the non-physical world who are also watching over him and trying to reach out to him. They are there loving him, even if he can't feel it. The love of God, of Source, is still there, always there, available to him. It is washing over him 24 hours a day, whether you can see it or not. And there are the physical people, as well, there to take care of him.

You are not leaving him alone. He is never alone. As the dementia progresses, you may see him open to more connection. The staff, of course, may or may not believe that the dead relatives or "angels" he is speaking to are actually present. That is going to vary according to their experiences and belief systems.

He is not alone. It is all right for you to leave. From his non-physical perspective, he is appreciating your love and your visits. He wants you to move forward with your own life. In his own way, that is what he is doing, too.

«« Q »»

My mother seems so frail, so vulnerable. I keep seeing images of her in my mind long after I have left the nursing home. It tears me apart inside.

Sometimes, the biggest challenge with our aging loved ones, or loved ones who are ill, is to remember who they really are: the essence of them. It does not serve them when we think of them as they are in these present moments. It *does* serve them if we remember who they really are, even if that authentic self is something they have not experienced in a long time.

When my mother's health declined seriously, I found a photo of her as a child, sitting high in the branches of a tree. She looked happy and full of life. I blew the photo up, framed it, and kept it where I could see it frequently at home. It reminded me: this is the essence of who she really is. She is the little girl who climbed trees, who hated to wear shoes and went barefoot everywhere. This is the little girl who loved to have fun, and smiled easily. This is the little girl who used to sit her younger brother down on the floor amidst her dolls and stuffed animals and pretended that she was a teacher and they were her students. She loved to play school. She loved to read. She loved to inspire and make people happy. She loved to tell stories. She loved to love.

That is the essence of who my mother is. Years of resistant thought had caused her to be where she was then. But who she really is, her essence, her authentic self, is not the self that was in bed at the nursing home. Her spirit is the

133

same; she had just grown separated from it. It became my job to remember who she really was. It became my job to see the image of the little girl when I thought of my mother. It became my job to remember her essence, even though she wasn't feeling it strongly anymore.

I knew that when she returned to her non-physical perspective, she would be that essence again. She would be fully herself: powerful and strong and able to climb any tree. She would be able to laugh easily and love easily and find reasons to be happy easily.

See if you can find photos of your mother. If you don't have photos of her early years, see if you can remember stories she or other family members might have shared. Ask relatives. Or simply go to a playground and look at the children. Look for a little girl who looks like your mother. Watch her enthusiasm. Watch her play and have fun. Remember that your mother was like that once, too, and that is the essence of who she is: loving and joyful.

When your mother makes her re-emergence to the non-physical realm, you will find it easier to connect with her if you remember her essence instead of this image you see of her at the nursing home. Look at the photos and memories of her as a child. Hold those in your mind and your heart. See her as she really is.

«« Q »»
I have just been given a diagnosis that I am in the early stages of dementia. What can I do?

I am going to address this from a spiritual, not a medical, perspective. You need to confer with your physicians for the medical perspective. From a spiritual perspective, the first thing is to find joy and happiness in your life, wherever you can. Make sure you create joy every single day. Live joy. Find memories that serve you. Create new ones. Be happy.

Second, make peace with death. There is nothing to be afraid of. You are going to a place of profound love and happiness. You are going to experience amazing, wonderful emotions and circumstances. Imagine yourself wrapped in the loving embrace of a God who adores you. This is death.

Third, create. Humans are powerful creative beings. Find things to make. Find things to do. Find experiences that make you happy. Whatever you enjoy in life, spend time doing it. Whatever you like to make, do that. If you have not tried artistic or creative pursuits in the past, do it now. Whether it is art, gardening, woodworking, writing, dancing...the list is long...be creative. Have fun with it. Don't postpone your joy.

You don't need to worry about your diagnosis. It is just a snapshot of where you are right now. And that can change. But being afraid of this diagnosis does not serve you or your family. Find joy in the present. If there are things you are worried about, find a way to make peace with them or to release the anxiety. Approaching this diagnosis with fear will not serve you.

Dementia often teaches people to live in and from the present moment. Within our culture, the diagnosis is often experienced as a type of death sentence. Death is a wonderful state of being, so there is nothing to fear. A "death sentence" is actually a sentence to happiness. Your physical separation from your loved ones is temporary, so you don't need to worry about losing them or the connections you have with them. An often overlooked benefit of dementia is that it teaches unconditional love: you loving yourself, and your family learning to love you just as you are in the present moment.

You need to understand that well-being is the norm, and that is the condition to which you will eventually return. As much as possible, find well-being now. Find happiness now. Find it with yourself. Find it with your family. Don't stop living out of fear. You can continue to create wonderful experiences and memories with your loved ones. You can model for them how to embrace this physical experience as someone who really understands. Live life to the fullest as long as you can. Many people find that the more they live, the slower the dementia creeps in.

Remember that your relationships with your loved ones are eternal. The relationships may change in the present moment if the dementia takes hold, but those relationships and the love you share are nothing to grieve because they will continue.

Tell your loved ones that you are taking an adventure into the present moment. Try not to worry about where this diagnosis might take you. You are in charge of your life now.

Find the fullness of the present. Look for the value in being together now. Be in the now. Find happiness now. Find love now. And you will find greater joy and peace than you ever expected.

Chapter 8
Allowing the Process

Unconditional Love, Happiness and Freedom

The more your loved one with dementia can experience these three things in his or her life, the happier he or she will be: unconditional love, happiness, freedom. It is also common that the more of these things your loved one has, the slower the dementia may be to progress. Now the progress of dementia is very personal, with many variables. But the more unconditional love, happiness and freedom your loved one has, the less quickly the dementia is likely to strengthen. Or, the more quickly your loved one will, happily, re-emerge into heaven.

Greater degrees of separation from the past in dementia are not always a bad thing, although we have come to see them that way. "Progress" in dementia can mean feeling happy and enjoying momentary well-being. It has nothing to do with memory. As someone becomes more separated from earthly life and his or her past, there is also greater connection to the non-physical. That is not progress we can necessarily see, but it is progress nonetheless.

Understanding Death

Dementia has existed for thousands of years. As long as humans have aged and not understood death, or resisted our natural expansion and "recycling," dementia has existed.

There are many reasons that it seems to us to be more common. One of these reasons is that people have less contact with death now and more fear of it. Death has become removed from us. When people had farms and raised animals, they knew there was a cycle to life. Even then, they may not have understood death. But they made some type of peace with it. They had to, in order to kill animals for food.

Death has become removed, remote, and sanitary. When people die, their bodies are removed, usually by strangers, and cleaned up. We see them later in coffins at funeral homes. Or their bodies are cremated and we receive their cremains in a sealed urn.

I grew up listening to my mother talk about how, when she was young, the families prepared the bodies of their loved ones who had died. The bodies were washed and dressed, coffins were brought into the house, and people sat up with the bodies of their loved ones around the clock until they were taken to the cemetery and buried. My mother talked about the impressions she had formed of death as a child. She said it was actually great fun sitting up with a body and the watchful adults at night. There was storytelling and good food. Memories were shared, and people laughed as they reminisced about the fun times they had with their loved one. She called it a great adventure.

When my father died, I was determined that we would prepare his body – that his own family would dress his body and prepare his body to be cremated. I still remember how therapeutic this was for me. As my brother and I tried to put clothes on him at the funeral home, it became so clear to me that my father's spirit was gone. We were dressing the shell he had lived in, not him. He was no longer there.

People grow up with all kinds of ideas about what death is, and most of those ideas are misconceptions. These concepts may come from individuals and institutions that are very well-intentioned. But today, more than ever, many people have fear around death.

Many people face death with terror – not love, not understanding, not acceptance. Since it is inevitable we die, doesn't it make sense that we make peace with death early in our lives?

As people approach a state of being that they dread and don't understand, isn't it logical they would adapt to try to find a way to cope with it? Let's say I had to fly on an airplane, I had no choice in the matter, and I was terrified of flying. I had such fear that I thought that my life was going to end – absolutely end – once I set foot on that plane. Wouldn't it be natural to assume I was going to be in a state of crisis as the date for that flight approached? We understand that, and yet we have less understanding, often, as people approach the state of death they have come to fear.

What does death mean to them? Is it a state of endedness, no state of being at all? Is it a time when they believe they are going to be judged for a lifetime of actions and thoughts, and possibly be sent to burn in a fiery hell for eternity? These beliefs allow for no control at all over one's approaching destiny, not at this late stage of physical life. If you really believe that something nightmarish is going to happen to you when you die, wouldn't you resist dying as long as possible? Of course you would.

Let's say you believe you are probably going to heaven, but you fear you may never see your loved ones again. That would be pretty scary. It would be frightening to think of leaving the people you love behind, and not knowing if you were ever going to be together again. Or even worse, deeply believing you wouldn't be together again at all. Maybe you believe they will go to heaven, but you don't know what is going to happen to you.

Even many religions that teach about heaven don't give specifics about what life is like there. One of the questions I am frequently asked by people is if they will be able to find their loved ones in heaven, because they want to be reunited with them. The answer is: of course. But most religions teach a vague concept of heaven – it is a really good place and you want to go there – without addressing concerns. So even if people believe they are going to heaven when they die, they still have many questions and few, if any, people to turn to for answers.

It can be hard to have faith on your deathbed. Even if it is all you have.

Dementia is not a dis-ease. It is the process of returning to a state of ease, first, and then re-emerging into the bliss of heaven.

Please let me go

Another factor that can affect someone with dementia is the willingness of those around him or her to accept that this person is on a journey that will climax with departure from a physical perspective, a body, and a re-emergence into heaven. No one can keep a person from dying. However, we can influence someone and the process the individual is going through.

If someone understands that he or she is going to die soon and leave the body, it helps if the people close by accept this fact. What sometimes happens is that the people close by determine they are going to "fight" death. They are not going to accept, with grace, that their loved one is going to leave his or her physical body soon. So even if their loved one has made peace with this, family and friends may not have.

While the family cannot keep the person there against that person's will, if someone has dementia and the family is fighting dementia, fighting death, then it becomes easier to move into dementia more readily. If the people around you don't accept what is going on for you, you want to relinquish the battle. It is easier to emerge into a mental state where you do not feel the emotional pull and demands of your family. Your body may still be present, but you can be easing yourself away from the struggle.

Helping the family prepare

Dementia can also, though, help a family ease into the idea of death, into the idea that their loved one is moving away from connection to the physical body. When a loved one enters death from a state of vital living, the family can be in a state of shock. But when someone enters death from a state of dementia, the family is often more prepared. They may not feel like their loved one has been present with them for a while, even a very long while. The feelings they have had in dealing with dementia may help to prepare them for the time that their loved one more fully leaves the connection with the physical body.

Dementia may not just help a loved one deal with death; it can also help the family come to terms with the upcoming change, with the impending death of someone they love and care about. People with dementia can become a different version of themselves. While you may grieve about one version of the person that seems gone, another version is right there with you.

Resolving conflict

Dementia can also help someone who is dealing with personal turmoil about the end of his or her earthly experience. From a more expansive God-like perspective, the person's life is viewed with appreciation and love. But some people come to the end of their earthly experience with negative feelings like regret or anger. Since they don't know they will return and have many other opportunities, they may feel like they failed with what they perceive as a single opportunity for an earthly life. There may be things they wanted to do or achieve, and they now feel they have failed. As opposed to a sense of fulfillment and completion, these people might feel that their earthly life is incomplete and unsatisfying – or worse. They may feel like they have let

141

their family down, let themselves down, even let God down. Dementia helps people let go of these feelings and ease into a state where one is gentler with oneself. Dementia can help ease the internal turmoil and conflict these individuals are feeling.

Likewise, if there is unresolved conflict with family members or others close to this loved one, dementia is a way of letting go on the journey to death. Your loved one may not see any way to resolve the conflict, yet a part of him or her wants to resolve it. Dementia is freeing. If a person can't find a sense of resolution with loved ones, then the dementia separates the person from the conflict and from the inner turmoil. It provides ease into a state of peace.

Humor

Dementia can bring a lot of happiness – not just to the people experiencing it, but to those nearby. I know this statement will seem like sacrilege to some, and to others, just insensitivity. And it is certainly not true of all people at all stages of dementia.

But some of the funniest things I have ever observed or heard have come from people with dementia. It can be like watching children. There is innocence. There is also an ability to laugh at oneself, and to enjoy when others around you are laughing – even at something you did. Some people with dementia enjoy entertaining others with their antics. If they do something that brings joy to others and they are aware of it, they may do it again and again, just like young children do.

If you can learn to laugh at these things – and to realize there is nothing wrong with the laughter – it makes life easier and more enjoyable.

I can remember calling my mother on the phone at her nursing home to tell her about a television show I thought she would enjoy. She had moments of clarity and not-so-great clarity at this point. I was telling her to turn the television to channel 12. So she would take the telephone and press 1-2 on the handset. She was pointing the phone toward the TV. The TV would not respond, so she would press 1-2 on the phone again. And again. Because she was pointing the phone at the TV, it was away from her ear. She could not hear me calling to her. And I kept hearing the buttons pushed, 1-2, 1-2, 1-2, in my ear. The television was just not cooperating!

So I clarified to her: let's find the silver remote control for the TV. She did. Once she got that in her hand, she could hear me telling her to press 1-2 on the silver remote and to point the small end of the remote toward the television. After a few tries, this was accomplished. When she realized what she had been doing, expecting the phone to control the television, she started laughing.

I found that my mother's hallucinations and dreams were a great benefit to me in telling me where she was emotionally. Since she could not always tell me how she was, her hallucinations and dreams spoke for her.

Emotional Indicators

Hallucinations, delusions and dreams can be helpful indicators of what is going on for someone emotionally. Emotions lie on a continuum, from those that feel worst to those that feel best. The emotional content of what someone reports seeing will indicate to you what the individual is feeling. The brain tries to make sense of what the eyes see and interprets it. There is a parallel between the interpretations the brain offers and what someone is feeling. They are usually on the same emotional frequency.

If my mother was feeling vulnerable and afraid, she might hallucinate about people sneaking around outside her window. If she was seeking comfort, she might dream about a church service. If she was happy, she might hallucinate about a dance with women in beautiful dresses. It was not the actual details of her dreams and hallucinations that mattered to me. It was the feeling she received when she had them, and how she was feeling as she told me about them. Whether these were dreams or hallucinations or memories from her own past, she was experiencing them now, in the present, as real.

I could talk with her about the dance, and she could describe the dresses to me that the women wore. She could tell me about fun things that happened at the dance and what a good time she had watching. I knew never to challenge her, or try to diminish her experience. She was living in a different reality than I was. If she was afraid, I could reassure her. The only times I would try to "straighten out" a perception was if something troubled her. But it usually worked best to "straighten it out" from inside her reality, instead of trying to overlay my reality onto hers.

I found that sometimes I could project myself into her hallucinations and make suggestions. For instance, she might be looking at an empty yard at a nearby house, but overlay an entire scene on it. If she was "seeing" children on a playground who were being abused by an adult, I could interject a police officer coming into the scene to arrest the perpetrator. "See the police officer, Mom? Look at the police car arriving. The police officer is here to protect the children and make sure they aren't hurt anymore." If she would allow herself to "buy in" to my projection, she would find relief. And helping her feel better was my intent.

The dreams and hallucinations of people with dementia are important indicators of what is going on internally for them. They can tell you what your loved ones are feeling. If it is an unhappy emotional point, you can work with them, gently, to try to help them feel better. If they indicate happiness, you can appreciate that your loved ones are having a wonderful experience. Appreciate happy hallucinations. Try gently to raise the emotions indicated by unhappy experiences for your loved ones to a better-feeling place.

But also know that the emotions that dominate are where individuals with dementia are going to return. I might help my mother feel better for a few minutes. But she would eventually return to the emotions of fear and vulnerability that dominated many days of her later life.

Also, some people will not let themselves be happy. No matter what you do, the story they tell of their lives keeps them miserable, and they are not willing to change it. Sometimes the unhappy part of life they talk about is a tiny part of the entire picture. If you try to cheer them, they will be resistant and fight you.

I have heard many people with dementia tell the family members who lovingly cared for them that they have been "abandoned" and forgotten, even if the family members were providing round-the-clock care. As a caregiver, you cannot take what feel like accusations personally. It doesn't mean you aren't doing enough. Sometimes, there is just nothing more you can do.

Compassion can play a valuable role when working with someone who has dementia. It was important for me to understand that my mother's feelings were not my responsibility. I might feel better if she is feeling better. It is natural I would want her to be happy. But already-happy people who understand and accept death and don't resist it, who flow with life instead of trying to control it, also don't tend to develop severe dementia or stay in a state of dementia for a long time before dying. My mother came to this state of dementia because she was already not happy. She was happier than many people at her age and in her physical condition. But she was far from the joyful, loving, free being that was and is at the essence of who she really is. That separation had been occurring for years, before the dementia ever started.

Letting go of attachments

One of the many interesting experiences I observed with my mother was how, with her dementia, she released her attachments to people she loved and had known for many years. At first, it was not through forgetting. It was through a loosening – and a lessening – of contact with them. When I was with her, I would ask her if she would like to talk to someone on the phone. I would name some of her favorite people: friends and family she had known and loved for many years. No, she did not want to talk with them.

Now, if these people called her, she would be thrilled and delighted about speaking to them. She would tell me for days or weeks afterward about these people calling. But *she* did not want to initiate contact – and she did not want me to initiate contact on her behalf.

Sometimes, it was because these people were undergoing health or personal challenges, and she felt it would be depressing to talk with them. There was nothing she could do to help them. If she was in a better-feeling place, she would not want to talk with someone where the conversation might be depressing. That is natural, of course.

At other times, I suspected the conversation would require a great deal of energy and focus from her. If you are in a gradual process of letting go of attachment to your physical world, it can be challenging to stay focused for even ten minutes. It can be exhausting.

She also "let go" of activities she had enjoyed for many years. Reading novels had been a favorite activity of hers. Now, she could no longer keep track of the characters and plots that she used to enjoy. She needed to let go. She had difficulty focusing on word puzzles. She would lose track of the details in movies. The best movies to watch for her were light comedies where she could react to a funny line or action, but where she did not have to maintain any memory of the story to enjoy the movie.

Before she developed dementia herself, my mother used to tell me that light-feeling children's cartoons and animated children's shows were the best thing for people with dementia to watch. She encouraged other residents of retirement centers where she lived to let their spouses with dementia watch children's programming on television. She noticed that when their spouses watched shows like *Dora the Explorer* or old *Peanuts* movies, they became more alert and lively – at least for a while – if they were still at a stage of dementia where they might react to outside stimulation.

Sometimes, one may not notice any physical signs of people paying attention to a program or movie. But watch the eyes. Are their eyes going toward the television screen? If they are not watching the screen, are they listening? Do you notice any physical changes in response to the program? The other factor that has to be considered is the commercials. Particularly on channels for mature adults or "seniors," some commercials are intended to produce fear to sell a product such as a medication or medical service. These types of commercials do not usually produce a good feeling in a person with dementia. So even if your loved one is enjoying the programming, be aware of the types of commercials – if any – running on the television channels. See how your loved one reacts, if at all. Negative commercials can undo the positive effects of watching enjoyable programming, so be sensitive to it.

147

Chapter 9
A Return to Ease

Because dementia is a process that unfolds over a period of time, you will be interacting with your loved one at its various stages. This process belongs to your loved one. While there are many factors that will determine its length and its degrees, the primary determinant will be your loved one.

Your role is to support your loved one and to allow the process to unfold. This is an evolving, changing process. You may witness many degrees of separation as your loved one moves to a softer focus and eventually a withdrawal of focus. If you resist this process, if you decide to fight it, you will make it harder on your loved one. Fighting this process is the selfish thing to do. The most loving act you can do, that you will need to recommit to many times, is to allow.

Ultimately, you have no choice but to allow. You cannot control another person's process. But you may think, in the beginning, that you can try. You may even think you *should* try. Remember that your loved one is attempting to move from a state of dis-ease to a state of greater ease, from a state of resisting to a state of allowing. This may also be your process. You need to allow, not resist, this process. If they want to fight and ask you to help, of course you can choose to assist them. But if they are not resistant, be aware if you are the one who wants to impose a fighting spirit upon them or grows frustrated that they are not fighting, in your eyes, hard enough.

Have you ever tried to control another person? First, you usually learn that you can't. Anything you view as a "gain" is usually undone through another measure. You can influence. You can inspire. And most importantly with this person who means so much to you: you can love. You can love unconditionally. You can love, accepting who this person is. Loving this person means you will witness various moments on the journey. You may not always love the journey. But this is your loved one's path, not yours.

Because your loved one is on this journey does not mean you will eventually take this path, too. Many people worry, for example, that having a parent with dementia is an indicator they, too, will "end up" with dementia someday. That is simply not accurate. There are many factors that have brought your loved one to this place. While we all eventually arrive at the same destination – our heaven, our home – there are numerous paths there. No two are exactly the same. When you see your loved one with dementia, you are seeing your loved one's journey. You are not seeing your own.

Surrender to the idea that this is your loved one's journey; it is not yours. You may walk alongside at times. But your role is to support, not hinder, progress. You may be a companion on this path at moments, but you cannot climb inside the internal experience your loved one is having. You can allow. You can love. This is a journey where focus will soften, thinking will grow less intentional and clear, and communication will lessen as your loved one withdraws from life on earth, and prepares for a fuller and happier life in the non-physical realm.

A Process of Rewinding

The process in which they are engaged is like rewinding: rewinding to times earlier and earlier in their lives. Mentally, they may become more focused on the past, on memories and associations from earlier and earlier in their lives. My mother, for instance, would get confused about who my brother was. She knew he was a beloved male family member, but she might call him by her husband's name, her brother's name, or his own name. She might say to me in conversation, when referring to my brother, "Who do I mean...Bob, Lynn or Mark?" She would often refer to me as her mother, not as her daughter. And then came the times that she did not know me at all. I knew I should not feel hurt by this, or even upset by it. I tried to look at it as an indicator that she was making progress on her journey, and that this was a new experience.

My mother would often see me as a benevolent stranger who was being kind to her, but who she did not know. I can remember one evening when I brought her a chocolate milkshake. She was living in a nursing home at this point: she required two people physically to transfer her from her wheelchair, as well as around-the-clock availability and assistance. With the stimulus of the milkshake, she started telling me that her daughter liked ice cream. And even though I gently interjected that I was her daughter and I was there now with her, she could not maintain the association. She went on to tell me about her daughter and son and how good they had been to her through her many illnesses. I thought afterward: this is a moment not many people have an opportunity to enjoy, to hear your loved one talk about you as she truly feels, describing you to what she perceives as a total stranger. Most of us don't get to experience it. I felt blessed that I did. So, yes, there are adventures for all of us when a loved one has dementia, and there are new treasures to be found along the way.

The process of rewinding is as physical as mental. People who stay on this journey a long time may return to a state of childhood and even infancy, both mentally and physically. Not everyone with dementia will return to this state of being. But many do. Gradually, a person may no longer be able to make complex choices, then simple ones. They may not be able to choose clothes or dress themselves. They eventually surrender being able to eat and drink and toilet themselves. They may return to a state of infancy, where all care has to be provided for them. They will leave this world as helpless and unassociated with it as when they first arrived. Like the infant who is beginning to focus on life on earth, the adult with dementia is gradually relinquishing focus.

My mother was as attached to life on earth as anyone I ever knew. Even though we had many conversations about death earlier in her life, she had endured enough hardships that she said she "did not ever want to come back." I reassured her that she did not make that decision now. But she was adamant. And so her idea of "this one time" attached itself in a struggle to hold onto what was here, or so I interpreted it. My mother loved life on earth. She didn't want to let go because she so enjoyed it. And while there were many things she still wanted to do, she did not seem able to comprehend, even pre-dementia, that she would have multiple lifetimes to continue to enjoy them, and could even have many of these experiences once she had re-emerged back into heaven.

Spending time with your loved one on this journey

For some people, spending time with their loved one is a wonderful experience. If your loved one with dementia is happy and joyful, you may look forward to times you can spend together. When people with dementia return to truly child-like mental states, they can be a lot of fun. If you are providing home care and also working full-time outside the home or tending to the needs of children and grandchildren, you may feel stressed and overwhelmed by attending to your loved one's physical needs. If you are very busy in your own life, you may feel like spending time with your loved one is an obligation. If your loved one is not happy and joyful, then it may seem difficult to you to find those quality moments. I urge you to be creative, and let go of preconceived ideas about what those moments should be like.

At my mother's nursing home, family members would often take their loved ones outside on (usually slow) walks, whether the loved one was walking, shuffling, or being pushed in a wheelchair. The family members might take the time to point out happy, interesting things: look at the pretty flowers, look at the beautiful bird, feel the warm sun and the nice breeze we get to enjoy today. As you find these things, you get to enjoy them, too. Whether or not your loved ones can notice these things, they are probably enjoying the feeling you are creating through your appreciation of nature.

However, if you are taking your loved one on a walk only because you feel obligated, you are rushing and you want to get it over with, your loved one may respond to that feeling. To begin with, your loved one may not want to go with you. Perhaps you get irritated and think you want your loved one's cooperation with this nice thing you are trying to do. But your loved one may be noticing your frustration, or simply be in a different place emotionally. You have to be flexible with your desires and plans.

At my mother's nursing home, I found that joining in on Bingo and some of the other activities to be very rewarding. She could not actually play Bingo, but she liked the feeling of being with others in a group activity. I could play her Bingo card for her as we sat together at the table. I used plastic markers that were her favorite color: red. And I would notice her eyes lights up as more and more red markers covered her Bingo card. She was finding value in the experience. We were spending time together. She liked that I was there, doing this with her. In fact, it provided greater ease to her that I was marking the numbers and she did not have to try to track them mentally. She even commented that we were "luckier" when we played together: we had more called numbers and red markers on her card than when she played on her own.

Set aside the time you spend with your loved one as a gift you are giving. Then also try to find value in it yourself. If you see your time together as a gift, then it can be easier to relinquish "control" and time expectations. If I can freely give an hour today, then that hour will be for her. If I am still there and start feeling uneasy after 65 minutes because I have other things to do, it is time for me to leave. If I can only commit 15 minutes and still feel good about it, then my visit is 15 minutes. Your loved one would rather you came briefly than not at all. And your loved one would rather you came by choice than from obligation or guilt.

If you cannot go or you find it too difficult emotionally and you feel guilty about it, then consider finding a volunteer to visit or even hiring someone. This is not necessarily the easy way out: don't view it that way. Strangers may find great value in spending time with your loved one; let them. It can be easier for a stranger or non-family member to spend quality time because they do not have the attachments and history you do. I can remember aides I hired who would tell me what a delight my mother was and how much they enjoyed her. To be candid, they enjoyed her some days a lot more than I did. And she enjoyed the aides. They had not heard her stories dozens of time. They did not have emotional reactions the way I did.

Even if your loved one is in an assisted living facility or nursing home, you can still hire aides to go in and spend time with them, or have other volunteers help. The staff in these facilities can be wonderful, but they are charged with taking care of multiple patients. They do not have the time to spend one-on-one; don't expect them to. Your visits, the visits of family members, friends, volunteers, and hired aides can all supplement your loved one's quality of life. But also: your loved one's happiness is not your responsibility. They are still responsible for finding and creating their own happiness. You see them doing this mentally more and more as the dementia progresses. As their focus withdraws and softens, they don't want to focus as much on outside stimuli.

Focus takes effort. So don't try to force them to focus as they spend time with you. You might turn on the television or play soft music or read and simply sit there with them. Your focus does not need to be on them. We often think we have to talk or somehow engage. If your loved one is at a point in the process of dementia where he or she does not want to focus and focusing takes unwanted effort, then simply being present may be the best and easiest choice for all. My mother would sometimes want me to touch her or hold her hand when I was with her. She wouldn't care that I was reading the newspaper. She just wanted to feel me touching her. At other times, she might not want me close to her physically at all. I needed to "read" her cues and listen to my own intuition. Several days in a row might be the same, then at other times, every day was different.

As you watch your loved one go through this process, it may help you to consider the child-like nature to which he or she is returning. There are things our society deems inappropriate because these "elders" are in adult bodies. But their spirits may be very much like children. As you watch the 87-year-old who doesn't want to wear buttoned-up clothes, think about the two-year-old who runs around naked and happy to feel so free. As the 92-year-old only wants to eat ice cream or mashed potatoes with gravy, remember the three-year-old who feels the same way. The innocence and child-like qualities in which we find so much value in children are there again. Respond to the age of their spirits, not the age of their bodies.

I can remember one time when my mother, quite "progressed" in her dementia, had been given a blue pill by the nurse. Now this was, medically speaking, an important blue pill. The nurse had given her the pill and some water, and my mother assured her that she had swallowed it. Meanwhile, my mother had been drinking a chocolate milkshake – one of the few foods she would eat at this point. About 45 minutes later, my mother says, "Do you want some of this?" And she opened her mouth and stuck out her tongue with a fragment of the blue pill on it. I was surprised the pill could have lasted that long. I was a little concerned she hadn't swallowed it. But mostly, I was touched that she had been holding onto something she thought had value and she wanted to share it with me. It was thoughtful of her. It was sweet: an act of kindness. She wasn't asking me to get rid of the pill; she was, in her own mind, sharing something important. I thought about how many times a young child has offered me something of great value that I did not necessarily assign the same meaning to. So I assigned value to the act of kindness: to the meaning it held for my mother just as for a child. And my heart smiled.

Section IV: Continued Understanding

Chapter 10
Preparing to Die

People often make preparations when they are preparing to die. These can come in many forms. They may be conscious, as when someone has been given a terminal diagnosis by a physician and is expecting to die soon. Or the preparations may seem to be unconscious: the person may not talk knowingly about dying soon but still may be taking steps to get ready.

There are many variations to these types of preparing. Because they are unique to the individual and the life he or she has created, they will be different for everyone. I would like to offer some examples. Please keep in mind that these are not necessarily indicators someone is getting ready to die. Do not be alarmed, for instance, if you find people you love, or even yourself, undertaking these efforts. They can all happen for many other reasons. You are more likely to recognize these in hindsight after a loved one has died, as part of the process he or she was undertaking in preparation to leave this physical perspective.

Cleaning Out

Some people want to sort through the items they have accumulated in their lives. They may give items to people they want to have them. They may donate others to charity. Or they may simply wish to make a list of where they intend these items to go when they die. Other people may decide to leave a lifelong home and move into a retirement center, or a smaller home or apartment near family. These are choices the individual is making, as opposed to life circumstances or other family members dictating these choices. Family members and friends may not understand why these changes are occurring. Hopefully, they do not resist the efforts of their loved ones. In a few cases, as when a young person is preparing to commit suicide, family and friends may choose to intervene, having recognized this step as a preparation for an early death.

It should also be noted that downsizing is a natural part of the process of moving to a smaller residence, whatever stage of life. But being forced to downsize can be difficult if one is not emotionally ready to let go of certain possessions. When my parents started to downsize, they rented a storage unit. They could take what they needed into their apartment, but they did not need to relinquish control of items they were not ready to release. We maintained this pattern with my mother after my father's death. She had items stored at my brother's house, my house, and a storage unit at the time of her death. She was a saver and a collector. Even if she could not have the items with her, it provided her emotional security to know "her things" were still safe. She would periodically send us searching into old boxes which kept our organizational skills sharp. We downsized her belongings with each of her moves, but we knew emotional security took precedence.

Getting Personal, Business or Legal Affairs in Order

Certainly, preparing a will or creating a living trust is not an indicator that someone is going to die soon. But sometimes, a person who is getting ready to leave will decide it is time to get "affairs in order." This can be especially true if someone has been superstitious or resistant to creating these documents. There can be numerous documents involved: the will/living trust; assigning another person(s) responsibility in personal, business, financial, legal or health matters; a living will; powers of attorney. It may be deciding who will take over a family business or be promoted within a company as a successor to his or her position. In essence, it is preparation for a future change. Again, hindsight after this person's death is when this will most likely be seen as an indicator he or she was making preparations.

The Farewell Tour

I started nicknaming this "the farewell tour" after I discovered the pattern, and saw friends and other loved ones undertake it. I can also tell you that none of them undertook this consciously as a farewell tour. While, on a non-physical level, they were preparing to leave their physical perspective, these people did not recognize that fact consciously.

The "farewell tour" is when someone decides to visit, for a last time, closest friends and family members. This may take the nature of a physical tour: deciding, for example, to rent a recreational vehicle and travel across the country, stopping to visit children and grandchildren. It may be a series of events at home: barbecues or picnics or dinner parties where family and friends are invited. It may be someone visiting places that were meaningful to him or her in the course of a lifetime. It may be a party celebrating a significant life event, perhaps a special birthday or anniversary.

All of these events may happen in someone's life without any connection to an impending departure. But they may also be indications someone is preparing to leave. It is as if they are saying: you mean a lot to me, and I would like to see you one more time before I go. It does not mean: we will never see each other again. You will see each other again, but perhaps not through physical bodies in this earthly lifetime.

Personal Organizing

Sometimes, people will want to look over papers or photographs or other personal items accumulated in his or her lifetime. It is a way to renew memories of people, places and events, making a journey with the mind instead of the body. It is a way to rekindle memories, to reflect on life's accomplishments. I have seen people undertake major organizational projects, putting photographs in albums, or sorting and labeling them so that other people will know who was in the photographs or where and when they were taken. This can also be a wonderful activity for family members to help with: it can be a way to spend time with a loved one and learn more about his or her life, or your own. I found that, as my mother talked about her past, she would also bring up stories of my brother and me that I did not remember. I felt sometimes like I was learning as much about my life from her perspective as I was about hers. It was a reminder of how much we co-create these earthly lives together.

Resolving Regrets

As we prepare to die, we often want to "make right" situations not previously resolved. There may be encounters we had with people that we have continued to feel badly about, even if we have not spoken about them. There may be people we lost touch with, and we spend time thinking about them or even trying to contact them. There may be arguments or disagreements we want to resolve, or family members, friends or co-workers we did not treat well and want to treat better. Sometimes, resolution can be found. Other times, one or both parties may find painful feelings re-opened or ignited. Because one person may be ready to heal the past does not mean everyone involved is.

If you find yourself on the unresolved side of one of these conflicts after someone has died, try to focus on the intention of the person if he or she contacted you and not on the outcome. And remember that it is never too late to resolve these matters. Even if someone has died, you can still talk and find resolution. From where the person is now, this matter has been resolved. He or she in non-physical is seeing it from a loving position and can understand it from a broader perspective – how the two (or more) of you got involved and perpetuated it. The argument no longer matters. What matters to that person now, in heaven, is the love and common ground you once shared, and will again. So if you are feeling guilty about this type of situation, try to forgive yourself and the other person(s) involved so that you can move on with your own life. All you may need to do is let it go, and allow yourself to stop thinking about it.

Final Preparations

Another aspect of a physical life's conclusion that one may prepare for is the service and handling of the body: a ceremony, if one is desired or expected; the disposition and final placement of the physical body; the possible donation of usable body organs to suitable donors or even donating one's body to medical science. Indicating one's desires, or even preplanning and making arrangements, can be very helpful to both the person who is preparing to die and to his or her family or "survivors." However, many people are very resistant to this idea, and may not undertake arrangements or discussions of plans willingly. If you have a loved one who is preparing to die, try to honor his or her wishes. If she or he wants to talk about it, realize it is important to her or him and pay attention. If, on the other hand, the person is resistant, then you may want to discuss these issues privately, as a family, without that loved one present. Do not force the issue.

My husband thought caskets were much too expensive, and decided years in advance what casket he wanted and from where he wanted it procured. He knew where he wanted to be buried. My mother did not want a celebration of life service and would not talk about it. If I brought it up, she would repeat a saying I had given her years earlier: "I know, these services are for the living." However, when my father died, she ordered separate headstones for each of them and had her name and birth date engraved on hers at the same time as my father's information was engraved. She had both stones placed at the cemetery because she wanted the two stones to weather together. It was important to her that the coloring and natural wear pattern of the two headstones match. She knew that if her stone had not been placed until she died, the weathering of the stones could be different – and that was not what she wanted. There turned out to be eighteen years between the deaths of my parents: she was right.

Thinking about these arrangements in advance can be very helpful to some people. I have known some who were very specific, even about the clothes they wanted to wear in the casket. Tending to these details offers a feeling of control over death. Other people find resolution in knowing that they are "sparing" their loved ones from these decisions at the time of death. There is no right and wrong here. It is all a matter of personal choice. And it is important to realize that, if these arrangements are not handled as dictated after the loved one's death, there are no recriminations or hard feelings from heaven. Your loved one is going to realize and understand whatever had to be done or undone. He or she has other priorities now, and what happens or happened on earth after death may be appreciated, but it is not going to cause any heavenly unhappiness.

Chapter 11
Grief

Grief is a process. While we know there are similarities in the ways people grieve, there are also differences. It is important to recognize and respect these differences. Do not expect someone to grieve the way you do. Do not expect yourself to grieve differently than you find yourself experiencing.

I have known people who did not cry, and felt guilty because they could not cry. I have known others who would not let themselves cry because they felt that if they started, they would never stop.

I have known people whose loved ones did not believe in crying at funerals, so they felt it would be disrespectful to cry. And still others who cried almost non-stop for days.

Grief is not a competition. Greater grief does not mean greater love. Grief shown on the outside may look very different than grief felt on the inside but concealed. They both hurt, just the same.

Some people remove all reminders of a person in their homes. Others put up more. Some people put up roadside memorials they feel honor their loved ones. Others don't want any reminder as they drive by the place of the accident every day on their way to work.

There is no right way to grieve. And no wrong way.

No matter how much you love someone, no matter how much you believe they are still alive and close to you, death brings a change. The physical presence of someone in your life is gone. And that can be hard to adjust to. That can be hard to accept.

Perhaps you do communicate with your loved one every day. Perhaps you still feel him or her close. But you are not having the same physical experiences together anymore. Yes, perhaps you will in the future. But for right now, there has been a transition. The immediate physical presence is gone. It is okay to grieve. But don't feel you have to.

God never intended us to grieve. The more we stay connected to God and to our loved ones in the non-physical realm, the less reason there is to grieve. Life has changed, but it continues. The relationship has changed, but it continues. Your love together still is. Your relationship still is. This wonderful being can still have a presence in your life. You can still enjoy being together. You can still appreciate you have even more time together in your future. One chapter is over, and a new one has begun, but you are still in the same book.

Even understanding what I do about death, I grieved for my husband more than I ever imagined was possible. I felt my life was over when he died. When my mother made her re-emergence to non-physical, my grief was different because she had changed so in her final illness and the process of dementia. I had started grieving earlier, when she was still alive. Knowing how much happier she was after her death, I found it still hard but somehow easier.

I remember when my father received his diagnosis of being terminally ill. At first, they had given him six months to live. I felt guilty grieving his impending death when he was still alive. It felt like I was wasting energy anticipating the loss of him, when he was still right there in front of me. Those six months became five years.

I learned that doctors only guess, although they do their best. It is an art, not a science. There are many non-physical factors that interplay with the physical reality. My mother's six-months-to-live diagnosis turned into ten years. Who could have foreseen that the energy of her twin granddaughters, Katherine and Laurel, would inspire her? She wanted to see them grow up. She believed she had to stay in a physical body to do that. When her third granddaughter, Jennifer, was born, she became even more determined to live. Now she had three grandchildren to watch grow up. Who would have known that the loving and tender care of her daughter-in-law, Rebecca, would see her through one illness after another? My mother found enough joy in living, and enough people to live for, that she was not willing to let go. She held on tight.

The most important thing to remember as you go through the process of grief is to be kind to yourself; be gentle with yourself. Don't expect too much of yourself too soon. Don't develop expectations of yourself based on what society says you should do or feel. Trust your own process. Allow it.

Follow your intuition about what feels right. If there is something meaningful you want to do, and it doesn't harm anyone, you may want to listen to yourself. Don't act out of anger. Don't act out of revenge.

I have known people who wrote letters to their loved ones after they died, to try to resolve remaining issues or say words that were never spoken. Some people tuck letters into caskets, toss stones into the ocean, or release balloons into the wind. Parties can be thrown in celebration of the loved one's new life.

I have seen photos framed and photos burned. People have visited cemeteries with picnics and wine, or stood on the grave and shouted. There is no right and wrong to grief. It is about what moves you *through*. What advances your feelings through the process of grief and returns you to focusing on the living, and on your life. You will never forget this person. You will never lose your love. But grief eventually needs to belong to the past, not the future.

Grief is about healing, and eventually, letting the past be the past. You are here to have a future. Your loved ones in non-physical may be a part of that. But they want you to enjoy a future that is based on joy, on meaningful connections with other beings having a physical experience. Continuing to grieve does not honor them; it dishonors you.

And it dishonors their wishes for you from the non-physical realm, to move forward and find happiness with new people in your life. When someone leaves, it makes room for someone else. The lost experiences and expectations make room for new experiences and expectations.

Honor your loved ones. Honor your self. Let the future in.

Chapter 12

Forgiveness

Why have a chapter about forgiveness in a book about understanding death? To some of you, the reason is obvious.

You may be angry with your loved one who has died. You may be mad at the person for dying. You may be angry you have been left alone.

You may have learned things about your loved one since the death that have made you angry.

Your loved one may have done things when alive that made you angry, but you did not let yourself feel the anger until after the death.

There may be many reasons you are angry. And that is okay.

You may also feel your loved one was angry with you at the time of death. The last time you spoke, you may have had cross words.

You may be feeling angry or feeling guilty. You may feel guilty for things you said or did, or things you didn't say or do but now wish you had.

Your loved one, in heaven, has forgiven you. In fact, your loved one is now seeing you, and those situations, with much more clarity and love. Your loved one has a broader perspective over what happened. Your loved one actually doesn't need to forgive because, from this new enlightened perspective, your loved one doesn't see anything that needs forgiving.

The only person who needs to forgive now is you.

Perhaps it is your loved one that you need to forgive. Perhaps you need to forgive yourself.

There is freedom in forgiveness. You need to forgive to allow yourself that freedom.

Grudges hold you to the past. They do not let you move forward.

They hold you to old memories, to painful times and experiences. If you want happiness in your future and joy in your present, you need to let go.

Forgiveness does not mean telling someone that what he or she did to hurt you is or was acceptable. It means *letting go*: letting go of the memory, letting go of the pain, letting go of the anger, letting go of the hurt.

When, and if, the thought of it comes up again, gently remind yourself that you have let it go. Then focus on something else more pleasant to think about. Think about a positive quality your loved one had. Recall a happy memory the two of you shared. Focus on a different topic in your present life that you feel good about now.

If someone else brings up the past, just say, "I have let that go and I don't want to focus on it anymore." And then don't. Don't let someone else stir up pain that you want to release. Change the subject. Leave the room. End the phone call. Don't read the e-mail. Do what you need to take care of yourself.

If you were involved in someone's death, whatever role you may have had, realize that person has now let it go. That person is in a happy place, and is not focusing on how he or she got there. People in heaven don't see what got them to that happy place as a bad thing. People don't hold grudges in heaven. It wouldn't be heaven if they did.

You need to be loving to yourself. And loving yourself means forgiving. Loving yourself means letting go of past pain. Loving yourself means you stop being unkind to yourself or anyone else.

Deciding to forgive is the first step. Decide to let go. Decide to release whatever you are feeling badly about, and let yourself move ahead into a brighter tomorrow.

Chapter 13
Suicide

While many people kill themselves to relieve physical pain, many more die in an attempt to relieve emotional and mental pain. What is interesting about people who commit suicide is that, at their core, they know death will bring relief. While some may only be hoping for it, it is important to recognize their internal knowing that physical death will end their suffering.

It does not matter what they believe, or what their religions teach about death. When their souls leave the perspective of the physical body and re-emerge fully back into heaven, their relief is immediate. From the perspective of the physical body, they felt trapped and desperate. They saw no other way out of their situation. From the more knowing perspective available in heaven, they can see there may have been other options their human thought patterns were not allowing. However, the re-emergence back into the fullness of who they really are is joyful and freeing. They feel completely loved and accepted. The peace so elusive to them on earth is found. They move from total desperation to total bliss.

God, Source, does not view suicide as wrong. There is no punishment in heaven for people who kill themselves. They are not seen in heaven as ending their lives too soon. In fact, from the non-physical perspective, there must be an agreement of sorts or the suicide will not be "successful:" it will only result in an attempted suicide. Likewise, many people who attempt to kill themselves on earth are only seeking relief and can find no other way to get it. It is not that they want to die. They simply want the pain to stop.

That is the reason for most suicides. They want the pain to stop. Whether the pain is physical or emotional or mental does not really matter. It is pain. The suffering and anguish

171

become unbearable. They know there is relief in death. They can not stand the suffering anymore, so they "choose" the only option they see as bringing relief.

When someone you love dies through suicide – or you suspect it may have been suicide – it is important to focus on where that person is now: on the joy he or she is feeling. You may have very strong feelings of your own about this act. But don't try to "what if" the past. Don't try to think about other options you wish your loved one had considered, or things you might have done or said differently. Accept that your loved one is in a state of peace, and move forward with your own life. Yes, this may be easier said than actually done. But hopefully you can find peace in life as your loved one found peace in death.

Many people who kill themselves truly believe that the people around them will be better off when they are dead. They may have felt, when on earth, that they had let their loved ones down. They had disappointed them. They had failed them. They may have felt great self-loathing, or believed they or acts they had done were very bad or even evil. You don't kill yourself if you love yourself, feel good in your life, and see lots of options and choices available to you. Friends and family may feel this way about you, but it is not how you feel about your life. And with suicide, it is ultimately how you feel that matters. Suicide is a very personal choice.

What the person who has committed suicide does is present us with an opportunity, in death, to practice unconditional love. You may not love the fact that this person no longer has the perspective of a physical body. You may miss the physical companionship of this being on earth. You may feel the loss of the future you were anticipating with and for your loved one. What you can work on now is focusing your thoughts and feelings about this person on your love for him or her. You can remember this person's positive qualities instead of thinking about the way his or her life ended. Instead of focusing on the pain he or she was having prior to death or how physical death came about, think instead about the joy and freedom being experienced now. Your loved one is happy now, and your loved one wants you to be happy. Even someone who dies wishing ill to others immediately loses that intent and instead moves to wishing them well.

You cannot be in greater alignment with the unconditional love of God and wish ill for anyone. You cannot feel unconditionally loved and accepted and not be happy. You can only wish happiness and love for others, no matter what your relationship was with that person on earth – and no matter what that person on earth may have done or not done for or to you. Your loved one wants you to be happy now. He or she is. Try to let go of any negative feelings you are having and find a way to focus instead on love. It may or may not be a challenge to do. But you will feel much better and freer when you can find that peace.

Chapter 14
"Lost" Expectations

When we lose someone, or anticipate an early ending to our own life, part of what we grieve for is what we had expected, or hoped, for the future. When we have children, we often plan their lives out. We anticipate their education, career choices, relationships, and their children. We often build decades into their futures with *our* dreams. When the child dies, we do not just lose the child: we lose the future we had envisioned for that child and our own place in it. We lose the dreams we had for our child and the dreams we had for our own future with that child.

The same is true when spouses die earlier than we anticipated. Many, or even most, of our expectations for the future will never, can never, be achieved. So we lose the spouse and the dreams of our future together.

When parents die, we often feel like we are losing our past, but we may also feel we are losing any future dreams we held for them. If the relationship with our parents was not happy, we may have been holding out hope that we would eventually resolve matters. Perhaps the imperfect parents would become perfect later in life. Perhaps the parents who never told us they were proud of us, or loved us, would somehow find it in their hearts to say those things. Perhaps we hope that the people who were not perfect parents will become perfect grandparents. If the issue remains unresolved, we realize we are not going to hear, through their physical bodies, the apology or redemption we always longed for. Perhaps we had expectations of a happy future role for our parents in our lives or the lives of our children, at weddings, graduations, the births of our own grandchildren.

If we find out in advance that our lives are going to end earlier than we planned, we are not just coping with our own impending deaths. We are also thinking about all the life events and passages in our own lives and in the lives of our loved ones that we were looking forward to and now think we are going to miss.

The grief we feel for these lost expectations can be powerful and painful.

The best way to deal with it is simply to let these expectations go.

Many people grieve by reliving the death over and over again. They go through future time by constantly bringing up the physical loss again.

They may celebrate future birthdays and anniversaries, missed graduations and weddings, by continuing to focus on the loss and the absence of their loved one.

It does not do anyone any good to keep resurrecting pain. It does not pay tribute to your loved one to continue to grieve.

Acknowledging some of these occasions is, of course, natural. But focus instead on how much you love and value the person, and on how much they *are* enjoying these celebrations. Your loved one still attends special family occasions in spirit. Instead of thinking how much they would have liked it, focus on how much they *are* enjoying it. Don't think about the child or grandchild they couldn't see; think about how much they *are* enjoying those children.

When my brother retired from the military, my mother and I attended his retirement ceremony along with the rest of our family. At one point in the ceremony, my mother and I looked at each other and said simultaneously, "Dad's here!" We both knew it. We could feel him there. And we could feel his pride in my brother's achievement. My dad had left the physical realm seventeen years earlier.

At my wedding, we had the priest read the vows from the book that my father used when he performed weddings. (He was a minister.) I knew my father would be there, and I wanted to make visible to him that he was still a part of the ceremony. I knew it would be meaningful to him that we chose to have the vows read from his book. We wanted to include him and honor him. And we did.

My father's grandchildren were born after his physical death. People often talk about how much he would have loved his three granddaughters. I think about how much he *does* enjoy them. Because I know he is thrilled. I know he watches them and loves them. I just don't get to watch him enjoying them the way I would if he were still in a physical body.

That is really what we are talking about here. Your loved ones are still attending many of the occasions you think they are missing. They aren't missing a thing. We just don't get to see them enjoying the occasion the way we would if they were still in physical bodies. Don't focus on their absence: allow yourselves to feel their presence. Feeling them with you on those special days will allow you the sense of fullness you are looking for.

If you want to celebrate anniversaries and birthdays of your loved one, do something that is *fun* for you, not mournful. You can talk to your loved ones. But focus on happy times, not sad ones. You might say to your loved one, "Remember when we celebrated that birthday? What fun we had!" Talk to them about the good times you shared. That is much more meaningful to them than mourning that they are not there in a physical body. You cannot get close to your heavenly loved ones by grieving. Only by rejoicing can you truly connect with them.

If there are lost expectations that you are not ready to release, then reframe then in the future. You and your loved one can still travel to the places you always wanted to – when you are both in non-physical. You can still make lives together – again, in the non-physical and/or physical. Your lives together have not ended. One short segment is over. But there are many, many more to come. Expectations may need to change. But they are not lost.

Chapter 15
Places Honoring People

Many people like to have a place to visit when they are thinking of their loved ones. Often, this place is a cemetery or memorial garden, or somewhere a loved one's body or cremains are located. We are in physical bodies; we have a physical perspective of life. And even though our loved ones no longer have a physical perspective, sometimes it helps us to have a place we associate with them.

The non-physical realm can seem very nebulous to us. While our loved ones may still come close when we are thinking about them or talking to them, we usually do not see them. So it helps many people to have a physical place to visit, or to envision, where we can still imagine making a connection.

Many find a setting in nature to be comforting. The beauty of nature feels supportive of contemplation, peace and inspiration. Others want a place that was meaningful to their loved one, or where they spent time together. Some will choose a place they wanted to see together, yet never actually visited. Or perhaps you've moved to a new location and a spot that your loved one would have liked there feels best.

Only you can find a place that feels right. And it isn't important that you have a physical place unless you want one, and it is important to you in your healing journey.

If You Couldn't See the Body One Last Time

Many people who last saw their loved one alive, and can't see their loved one's body again, for whatever reason, may feel like they have lost an opportunity for closure. It may feel like their loved one has simply slipped away, vanished. Closure with the memory of that earthly body can still be achieved.

First, it is important to remember that your loved one separated from his or her body at the time of death. Your loved one no longer feels any connection to that body. His or her focus is on the present experience, not the past. It is not important to him or her that the body is found, that the body was not treated according to cultural or religious standards, that the body was treated violently, or that the body may have been "disrespected." It does not matter to your loved one, even if it matters to you.

It is also important to understand that many people who die violently leave the body before the worst of the violence. If they understand it is time for them to leave, they are not likely to stick around for the completion of a violent act. The body may still be alive for a time after someone has left. Residual energy, and the desire of the cells of the body to stay alive, may allow the body to stay animated and medically alive even after the spirit has left.

The moment of "death" may not be when the last breath is taken. It may come sooner. Some people in comas, for example, have left their bodies, even though the bodies are still alive and maintained by machines.

Where Your Loved One Is Now

Expand your idea of your loved one beyond the physical body he or she used in this life. Allow your thinking to embrace where he or she is *NOW*, and stop associating him or her with what has become the past.

You do not need a location to be present with your loved one, or to communicate with him or her. You can talk to your loved one *now*. You do not need a grave to sit by.

You may not have a physical place that you associate with your loved one, or it may be far away. If it helps you to move forward with your healing, then *create* a space that is meaningful to you. It might be as simple as a box you keep in your home of photographs and memorabilia. It may be a marker you place in a cemetery, without a burial. It may be a tree you plant or a bench you donate to a park. If you need a place, create a place. Do what is going to feel good to you and help you move forward in your own living. That is what your loved one wants for you: for you to be happy. He or she is now in a place of fully understanding that you will be together again. Moving on with your life will not seem disrespectful or unloving.

New Opportunities

I have known people who became closer to the person they loved after that person died. In earthly life, there were obstacles keeping them emotionally, or even physically, apart. In death, there are no obstacles. The lack of physical body does not need to be an impediment to a continued, close, loving relationship.

Death creates new opportunities for us, even as we may feel it takes away other opportunities. New doors can open: doors we may not have known were there before.

Create a space, if you need it, to find resolution with the past. Then let the past go, and reach out to the spirit of your loved one now, who is still alive, still loving you, still wanting and available to connect.

181

Chapter 16

Dreams

Dreams can play many roles in the process of recovering from grief. Sometimes they may feel like they exacerbate feelings you already have. You might dream about looking for your loved one who is deceased and being unable to find him or her. You might have a dream where something unfortunate has happened to your loved one. Dreams can manifest in many forms, expressing a variety of emotions.

Many people who have lost a loved one may also experience dreams that they find comforting, that even help them to move forward in their process of healing. For example, when my mother's only brother died, she had many strong feelings towards him. She was angry with him about issues that remained unresolved between them at the time of his death. She was angry he did not tell her sooner that he had cancer, or how invasive the cancer was. She felt he died too soon, and did not give her the time she needed to prepare for his death. She was, frankly, just plain mad at him.

Years after his death, when she was still angry with him, she had a dream where he came to her one night and the two of them talked. They talked and talked. She felt like they worked through all of the issues that had been unresolved at his death. They made peace, and returned to a place where they could express their love for one another. All conflict was resolved and dissolved. After this dream, she talked about her brother very differently; she felt very differently toward him. She was back in a state of fully loving him. Her anger was gone. This dream helped her immensely.

Another time after my father's death, her husband, my mother told me how he came to her one night while she was

183

sleeping and he just held her. She had been experiencing some frightening health issues. She said, "Your father visited me last night." She had been telling me how much she had missed him and missed his comforting touch. He also spoke to her and the two of them talked, expressing their love for one another. She felt great comfort from this experience.

A few months after my oldest cat died, I had a dream with her and another of my cats. The two of them had gotten lost during a storm and I found them safe inside a bookstore; I love bookstores and have always found them comforting. I had missed this cat. Megan had been with me more than fifteen years and followed me everywhere. When I sat at the computer writing, she lay behind the monitor. When I read, she sat on the back of the sofa, behind my head. When I cooked, she stretched out in the kitchen. In this dream, I could pet her and feel her long, soft grey fur. I could hear her unique "meow" as she spoke to me. I woke up feeling I had experienced a wonderful visit from her.

Whether these are dreams, ramblings of the imagination and mind, or actual visits from the spirits of these loved ones is irrelevant to me, and was to my mother, as well. They felt real. They moved us forward in our healing and in our living. And that is all that really matters.

If you have a dream about a loved one who has died, cherish the time you spend together. If you don't like something in the dream, go back to the dream – awake and conscious – and resolve it. Give the dream a different ending. Have a lucid experience where you create the conclusion you want. If your loved one leaves you in the dream, go back and see the two of you being reunited. If your loved one is lost, create a place where you find him or her. This is your dream. Give it the ending you want to have, that moves you to a place that feels better. Your loved one wants that for you, and you deserve it.

Chapter 17
Dealing with Grief:
Choosing Your Thoughts

I remember when I was at the cemetery and we were about to bury my husband's body. I knew that he was not in that body. He was no longer connected to that body in any way. But I had many fond associations with that body. I loved him in it. He was so handsome and distinguished. He had the most gorgeous white hair. And he was always proud of that body.

It was hard to know that I would not see that body again. Hard to know I would never run my fingers through his hair again. It felt impossible to think about not touching him.

And I realized: I need to choose my thoughts. I need to focus on the positive.

That body served him well. Very well. It was a beautiful body for him. Just perfect. It fit him so well. It represented him so well. And I loved him in it.

That body did just what bodies are supposed to do for us. What a great body that had been for him.

I could not focus on that body going in the ground. I could not focus on the fact I would never touch that body again. These thoughts would have led me to feel like I wanted to throw myself in there with him. I knew that. This is not my husband, I told myself. This was his body. A great body. But he is happy now. I need to focus on how happy he is now. I need to stay focused on his happiness, his freedom, his joy. I need to stay focused on how he is now, and not on what seems lost to me.

There were a few minutes when funeral officials had trouble getting the coffin to fit inside the burial vault the cemetery required. I found absolute delight in that, because it suited my husband perfectly. He had not planned,

185

consciously, to die yet. He wanted to live to be 100. And he was the most stubborn man I ever met. It was like the energy of his body had absorbed so much stubbornness, it wasn't going to yield to the idea of burial. At least, not yet. Not when it was not on his terms.

I thought, if my husband's spirit is here – and I felt it was – he is thoroughly enjoying this. He is having a great laugh. Perhaps he is even helping to maneuver this moment for my enjoyment. For my distraction. To bring my focus back to where he is now. I knew he would love this scenario. And that helped me to smile and laugh at it. Keeping my thoughts focused helped me to survive that burial.

Knowing that one does not "die" at death does not mean one does not grieve. Some people may not. But death does mean a change. It does mean a transition. Even if my husband is still very much "alive," he is not connected to his body anymore. None of us are ever as connected to our bodies as we might think. But knowing my husband is still alive, being able to communicate with him and know he is around me, still does not totally erase my grief.

What I did know was that I needed to choose my thoughts. I needed to stay focused. I needed to focus on what "is" and not on what "might have been."

Choosing one's thoughts is not as easy as it might sound. We tend to select most of our thoughts by default. We let people put ideas in front of us, through the television, computer, radio or in other electronic formats. We listen to people talk *at* us, without engaging in genuine conversation. And then we *respond* to those ideas.

Choosing what to think takes conscious work. It takes intention and effort. It takes practice.

It means realizing that I have control over my own mind. Thoughts do not think me; I think them. I choose them. Every single thought I have, I choose to think. No one implants thoughts in my mind. Only I control my own thoughts.

People may tell me things that I don't want to hear. But I don't have to listen to them. I can change the subject. I can excuse myself. I can tell them that I want to talk about something different – and then I need to do it. If they don't like it, they can walk away and probably will. I choose what to think. "Society" may have ideas on how I should deal with death, on how I should deal with grief. Only I know what is helpful to me. Only I know what works for me.

I talk about my husband in the present tense. This is odd to people. Sometimes I use the past tense just because it is the practice people in our society expect. But he is still alive. His spirit *is*, not *was*. He *is* still a wonderful, amazing man. I know that. Talking about him as if he is dead and gone seems somehow wrong to me – a betrayal of him, a betrayal of what I know. Some people think that means I am in denial that my husband is "dead." Well, that's okay. Because he knows, and I know, that he is still very much alive. He knows, and I know, that we will be together again. That is what matters.

Choose Feeling Good

Sometimes you have to work at feeling good.

It is easy just to observe what is around us. It is easy to let one thought lead to another like it.

You have to want to feel good. You have to *choose* it.

Grief perpetuates itself. You find yourself moving from one sad subject to another. You do not find relief.

Deciding to move from grieving to feeling good is a choice. It is an effort. It requires *focus.*

I have a path to joy when I think about my husband. I think about my favorite memories of him, my favorite memories of us. I think how happy I was when I was with him. I think about him being happy. I get inside that feeling of happiness. I take every aspect of that memory that provides joy and look for more. When I have moved fully into joy in my memories, then I think about where he is now: how happy he is. His joy now exceeds anything he felt on earth. He is in such a state of bliss. He feels loving and loved beyond his greatest experience here on earth. I can only feel joy knowing that. I stay focused on his state of bliss and love until I am feeling so good for him that I am feeling it, too.

In that joy, I feel closer to him. In that joy, I feel closer to love. In that joy, I feel closer to unity with him.

If you are having trouble communicating with your loved one, try the exercise I just described. Begin with happy memories. Get inside those memories. Feel that joy again. This exercise will take effort, especially the first few times you do it. But after a while, you will have created a path that will become easier to find and travel again and again.

Your loved one wants you to be happy. Your loved one who wants to communicate with you wants you to be joyful so you *can* communicate.

Grieving does not do anyone any good. It is not a tribute to your loved one that you grieve. Your loved one *wants* you to be happy. Your loved one wants you to know that you can be happy without him or her on earth. There is nothing at all wrong with that. It has only been through a misunderstanding of death that grief has become so painful.

Separation is temporary. It is, primarily, an illusion. You can still feel your loved one with you, and have experiences together, if you choose to and if you allow it. But as long as you are focused on what is *not* anymore, and what you now perceive as lacking, you will keep yourselves apart.

The irony in this situation is that your loved one wants to be close and wants you to know that he or she is close. It is your grief that is keeping you apart. Your loved one can't communicate with you directly if you stay in grief. You *have* to get happy. You *have* to want to feel good and get yourself into a place where you are feeling great in order to communicate.

Your relationship is eternal. There is no ending. There are no goodbyes.

Fairy tales are known for their final phrase: "and they lived happily ever after." There is a "happily ever after" awaiting each of us.

Our lives are eternal. We are eternal. Our joy is guaranteed. If not on earth, then in heaven.

When you finish reading a book, you might close it and put it down. But you go on.

You don't end because the book is finished. You might pick up your next book right away and start reading. Or you might wait a while.

The choice is yours to make.

Death is the "happy ending." And this "happily ever after" does come – every time, to each of us.

Fairy tale characters live "happily ever after."

And so do we.

Section V: Moving Forward

Chapter 18
A Loved One Lost? Where to Now....

If you are grieving the death of a loved one, it is important to stop and consider: what would your loved one want for you now? Often, we seem to put our lives on hold after a death. We may move from shock and bewilderment into depression and perhaps anger. Our lives can turn and focus on what isn't anymore, on what is not going to be. Our days and nights become filled – not with the love of this person, but with the loss of this person. Instead of focusing on the life that was lived and the moments we celebrated together, we instead think about the emptiness, the silence we feel: what isn't going to be anymore.

In their new connection to spirit in the non-physical realm, our loved ones want one thing for us: to be happy. They are not spending their days with "what ifs." They want us to be happy, as they are. They want us to connect with loved ones, and make new connections to bring more loving people into our lives. They don't hold any resentments or regrets. They want us to feel fully alive again: to feel joyful and enjoy life.

Regardless of what people say to you, don't "what if..." over the death of your loved one. Don't ruminate about how things might have turned out differently. Don't turn dreams that may not be realized into more grief about anticipated losses. Don't let well-intentioned people who say the wrong thing set you back.

Don't let the death of your loved one be the death of you. You have a right, indeed a duty, to move forward with your life. Your loved one wants you to.

It doesn't mean you won't "slip back" sometimes. It doesn't mean you won't have moments of sadness or tears. But let the general direction of your life be *FORWARD*. Don't let it get stuck. Don't try to recapture a past that is gone. Create new memories in your future.

What do you want in your life? How do you want your future to be? It really is okay to move ahead. Your loved one *WANTS YOU TO!*

Think of yourself as the captain of your own boat. We are still navigating the waters of our lives. Sometimes the water is smooth and progress is easy. Other times the water is stormy and we feel tossed about. Or the water might be rough but we move ahead anyway. A boat has a destination. Let yours be happiness. Let yours be joy. Pay tribute to your loved one by loving again. Love yourself. Love your life. Love new people who enter. Love.

Your loved one is living fully where he or she now is. You need to do the same.

Be kind to yourself. Be patient with your progress. Healing takes time. But let the healing begin.

Chapter 19
The Not-a-Conclusion

There is a new way to approach death and dying. Instead of looking at death as an ending, see it as a transition to a new chapter of life. That is, after all, what "death" really is. We leave the perspective of the physical body and we return to the perspective of our grander non-physical self.

Instead of being sad about this chapter ending, we can focus on our happiness and excitement that a new chapter is beginning. Dying is announcing, not just the closure of one chapter, but the beginning of another.

As I worked on the final draft that would become this book, my mother was lying in a nursing home, dying by human standards. I was not writing these sentiments from a philosophical vacuum. I was writing these words as someone who was in the middle of the process. I would sit by her bed as she slept and edit the pages. I could think of no place more real to the process of dying than where I was to ensure emotional integrity in this book.

To talk with her about this chapter of her life concluding did not bring her joy. To some people, it might. She knew this chapter was ending. But what made her happier was to talk about the next chapter.

There are places her body could no longer take her on this earth that she still wanted to visit. We talked about her traveling after her death, after she left this body. Where do you want to go? What do you want to see first?

There are many people and animals she loved who had already withdrawn from their physical perspectives and were exclusively in the non-physical world. We talked about them, about how great it would be for her to see them and be with them again. She was looking forward to seeing her husband again, and her parents, and her brother. She had a lot to talk with them about. She was looking forward to being reunited with the cats and dogs she had loved so much over the years. How great it would feel to be with all of them again.

We talked about future events on earth she might want to return for: her granddaughters' graduations, possible weddings. She knew she would be there. She would have the best vantage point in the building!

The conclusion of this book is that there is no conclusion to our lives. We write the stories of our lives. We conclude this chapter and begin a new one. With every ending comes a new beginning.

The people you love, that you have lived with in this chapter of your life, are people you will continue to play with in the new chapters, too. Goodbyes are temporary.

My mother's granddaughter, Jennifer, at the age of nine, was visiting her grandmother in the nursing home while her "Nonna" lay dying. Everyone understood what was happening. Jennifer said, lovingly and powerfully to Nonna: "Maybe you can come back and be my baby." Jennifer understands.

We do continue to play together, live together, laugh together. We do it in the non-physical world and in the physical world. We continue to write the stories of our lives *together*.

Our society teaches death as sadness and pain. So often, the pain of grief keeps us from feeling and connecting with our loved ones who are *right here with us*. The loved ones in physical bodies are people we can continue to create with in happy ways. The loved ones who have left their physical bodies are still alive and with us much more than we know. If we are in pain over our temporary situation, we cannot enjoy them. We cannot feel them.

Last night, the moon was full. It was a beautiful autumn evening, and I had gone outside to admire the brilliant moon and stars. I felt truly inspired. I felt my husband there with me, and almost without thinking about it, began dancing a waltz. I could feel my husband there with me, in the dance. We always loved dancing together. Some people might think I was simply feeling a memory. They might think I was crazy. But it was him. His spirit was there with me. I felt like I could have lifted my arms and felt his tall, strong shoulders. My Pat has been dead four years, and we danced a beautiful waltz together last night.

I was once visiting with an acquaintance who was sad that his friend had died. He and his friend were going to write a book together. He was upset there would be no book and no shared experience of creating the book together. But his "dead" friend was there, in spirit, and still wanted to write the book with him. My acquaintance's belief that his friend was no longer accessible to him was the only thing keeping them apart. They could still write the book. They could still co-create that happy experience.

So much of our suffering occurs from false beliefs. When my mother died, I knew people would say "I'm sorry" because that is what we say to each other in this culture. But consider: is there really much to be sorry about – that my mother is off creating a new chapter of her life? It is a lot like what happens at weddings for many parents. They are sad that a chapter of their lives with their son or daughter is concluding. But they are also happy that a new chapter in their child's adventure is beginning. The parent will not be as much a part of this new chapter as the last chapter. But they will still share many wonderful moments together. There are new joys to be created and celebrated because of this wedding, because of this new chapter. I do not know all of the joys that await my mother in this new chapter of her life, but I do know there will be many. Would you ever think of saying to a dear friend, "I'm so sorry your child is getting married?" Of course not.

We, in our misunderstanding of death, are the only reason that funerals are not as joyful as weddings. "Wow, Mom – a new chapter of your life is starting! How wonderful for you! We are going to celebrate the 'just-concluded' chapter you did such a great job of creating. Be sure to join us!"

What if, instead of saying goodbye, her granddaughters said, "Nonna, see you at our graduations! And our weddings! Come back and share all the life events so meaningful to us! We look forward to you being there!"

I invite you to look at death in a new way: the way God does. God knows there is no ending to us: we are eternally alive. When we look at this one physical life within the perspective of our eternal existence, death is simply about turning a page to a new chapter. The book of our lives does not end. The relationships with the people we love and care most about continue from lifetime to lifetime, chapter to chapter. We never say goodbye to each other. At most, we are saying, "*Until we meet again....*" Because we will meet again. And we will enjoy co-creating new experiences with each other lifetime after lifetime.

My mother's cremains were buried in her family plot in her hometown in the mountains of North Carolina, with her parents' bodies on one side and her husband's on the other. We had a graveside service that satisfied her wishes. No large service: just immediate family. We played and sang the music she loved. We read her favorite Psalm, 121. We shared thoughts and remembrances. Her youngest granddaughter, Jennifer, whom my mother always referred to as her sunshine, sang "You Are My Sunshine" to her Nonna. Her older granddaughters, Laurel and Katherine, shared their love as well. Her daughter-in-law, Rebecca, offered touching memories of Marie. My brother played my mother's favorite song on his trombone, just as she had requested: "His Eye Is on the Sparrow." This city cemetery was absolutely vacant while we were there, holding this service. My brother's trombone rang throughout the hills.

I could feel my mother there, with us, enjoying and appreciating our appreciation of her. I did not want to feel sad, as I knew I could not stay connected to her presence if I got caught in the grief. It was more important to me to be there with her, and feel her there with us. It was a powerful reminder to me that she is still very much alive, very much with us.

I realized how much wisdom my mother had gifted me through her experiences. She first became ill when I was a child, and was experiencing multiple physical challenges by the end of her earthly life. We traveled these paths together much of the time, although I know her journey was quite different from mine. Still, if it had not been the path taken, I would not have learned so much to share with others, and perhaps assist them as they follow similar paths. If I can help you find any relief, then please thank my mother as well as whomever who led you to this book. My mother paved the way for me to understand. Her experiences caused me to ask and ask and ask. My father taught me to ask and allow the answers. Divine Wisdom answered, and I have shared those answers here as best I could.

I know I have more to understand. We all do.

Death is a return to love. It is a return only if we have become separated from it. Which most of us have. Death is like rising into the most tender, loving, comforting embrace you have ever known. You return to a place where you are unconditionally loved, unconditionally accepted.

Dementia allows us to ease from fears and false beliefs back into a childlike NOW. It is a gradual releasing into allowing. It is a return to love.

The nature of the soul is eternal. The soul makes many journeys, lives many lifetimes. It is constantly expanding. It never, ever dies.

These are odysseys of love. Sent to us by God, by Source, who loves us always. Who knows we will always return home. Who knows we are never so far away that we can't hear, unless we choose to stop listening, choose to stop believing. God knows that we come from love, and that we always, always return home to love.

Feel the love of God with you now. And always. Know that who you are is cherished by God now, and always. Know that the joy singing in your heart will return soon, if not today. You are loved.

We are never alone on these odysseys. The more we attune to love, the more company we find on the trip. Life may be an adventure, but joy in death is guaranteed.

Be happy.

Be love.

Be the joy you come from and are returning to.

Our journey begins and ends

in **love**

every time.

With Loving Appreciation

I wanted to write this book for my nieces and others of their generation. I believe if we understand death, we stop living in fear of it. Fear less, live more. So I dedicate this to you, Laurel, Katherine and Jennifer. You are each amazing, and I live in love and awe of you. You inspire me.

I thank Dr. Mark and Rebecca Williams, my brother and sister-in-law, for their unending support and for the loving care they provided our mother. The conversations we shared about our mother's progressing dementia and the experiences we shared through her dying were invaluable.

I thank my mother, Marie Hall Crawley Williams, for her willingness to talk with me frankly and candidly about death and aging through the decades of her life. I appreciate her openness to talk about and explore "weird" spiritual and energy topics without judgment. I thank my father, the Rev. Dr. Robert John Lingenfelter Williams, for sharing his spiritual beliefs and his passionate thirst for knowledge. You both taught me that open minds and asking are a requirement for learning.

I thank my husband, Pat, for his unending love, his understanding of the value of freedom, and for his support which allowed me time to write. I offer deep appreciation to his children for the way they welcomed me into their family when we married: thank you Tenna, Cathy, Therese, and Andy. Thank you to my sisters-in-law, Julia and Mary Kathryn, for your encouragement and love. And thank you, Wanda Smith and Georgia Milam, for your support and the great care you took of Pat.

I thank the participants of my Abraham-Hicks book discussion group and Intentional Living group who encouraged me to write and were enthusiastic for me to progress. I appreciate your questions and the answers your asking inspired. I appreciate the passionate search for knowledge that we shared. I particularly thank Barbara C, Barbara H, Barbara S, Bob, Jeanie, Johanna, Korina, Lanni, Margaret, Mary, Nancy, Peggy, Raquel, Rene, Rhonda, Sue and Tonia.

I thank my friend, Dianne Jones, for asking me to give her a reading list on death. When I realized there was no one book that contained what I knew and wanted to share with her, I realized I should write one. I thank Fred and Susan Stewart for their enthusiasm about this project and, of course, Simon. I thank Elke Starke and Tresa Amrani for our hours of long, passionate discussion. I thank Joan Chandler for your enthusiasm about my previous book, which inspired me to publish this one. I thank Bob Lewellen for sharing your friendship and your candid thoughts about death and grief. I thank Susan Luks and Juli Burnell for our decades of loving friendship and thoughtful discussion. I thank Madhuvanti Kale and Vaishnavi Shekar for your wisdom, friendship and loving spirits. Thank you, Patty J, for the year of lessons on inclusiveness and graciousness that you have lived and modeled for a lifetime.

Thank you to Phyllis Braun and The Group for all the wisdom, insights and love you shared with me over the years. Thank you to Pam M., Linda B., and Cindy S. for your support at challenging times of my life. Thank you to Andy and Kim Jacobs for calling me a writer before I was willing to call myself one. Thank you to Rachel Kolcheck: it is always fun to share discussions of the writing process with a fellow writer. Thank you to Dr. Linda Wagner-Martin, my mentor for decades and the reason I chose to major in

English as a university student. I never understood, even as a student, how you wrote so much. You remain an inspiration.

I thank Nancy Baxter of Hawthorne Publishing who first read the complete manuscript and shared her wisdom and experience. Your encouragement and understanding were deeply meaningful.

Thank you, dear cats, for your patience while I wrote instead of petting or playing with you. Thank you for allowing me to finish "the next thought" before I fed you or let you out. Thank you for sitting behind my computer monitor while I typed, and in my lap while I edited.

Thank you, Leonore and Reddie. Thank you, J.E. and Flossie. Thank you, Mabel and Arthur. I appreciate your continued love and guidance.

Thank you for reading. Because if you are reading this book, then I have written it for you, too. I hope you can find the enlightenment you are seeking, and it is a stepping stone along your path.

I also want to share something along my journey that I have learned. Good memories are the only ones worth keeping. Whatever you are experiencing now, I hope you will *find the best in it and let the rest go*.

With deep and loving appreciation for all of you,

Graehme

December 2012

Notes

Odysseys of Love